Edward A Whitwam

Under the Old Flag, or, Memories of Field and Camp

Edward A Whitwam

Under the Old Flag, or, Memories of Field and Camp

ISBN/EAN: 9783337090593

Printed in Europe, USA, Canada, Australia, Japan

Cover: Foto ©ninafisch / pixelio.de

More available books at **www.hansebooks.com**

PROF. E. A. WHITWAM, D. D., LL. D.

UNDER THE OLD FLAG,

OR

MEMORIES OF FIELD AND CAMP.

PROF. E. A. WHITWAM, D. D., LL. D.
"BARD OF THE CAMP FIRE."

Late President McKendree College, President North Nebraska Normal College, Professor Hedding College. Author of Holding Down a Claim, Against Wind and Tide, Love All-Conquering, Etc.

COPYRIGHT, 1898.

E. A. WHITWAM, Publisher,
Abingdon, Illinois.

ENTERPRISE-HERALD PRINT,
ABINGDON, ILL.

PRELUDE.

The conflict is o'er, 'tis a thing of the past;
Our flag is unfurled o'er each state at last.
Still the patriot's pride, it has lost not a star,
And the ship of the union retains every spar.
Be ours the task once again to recall
Those sad, dreary days, when like a dark pall,
The black cloud of war hung heavy o'er all;
Come, march we again over field and through fen
To fight the old battles all over again.

DEDICATION.

To every man who wore the blue
   On mountain or in valley ;
To jolly tars, the seamen true
   Who sang aloud the rally,
When Farragut close to the mast
   Was lashed while fierce the battle
Waged hot, and shells both thick and fast
   Against the hull did rattle ;

To those who died ; to those who live ;
   To each who loved the banner
And dared, if need, his life to give,
   While marching with the Tanner ;
To Uncle Billy's bummers all,
   Who swept to the Atlantic
And hastened to its awful fall
   Disunion's scheme gigantic ;

To comrades all of former days,
   Who marched beneath Old Glory :
To those who, mid the campfire's blaze,
   Were wont to tell the story

Of each day's fights and fight them o'er,
    While cedar rails were snapping
And spitting fire from every pore
    Beneath the waving sappling.

To each dear girl we left behind,
    Our mothers, wives, intended,
To feed the cattle, corn to grind,
    And keep the fences mended.
To those too young when we went out
    To feel the darts of Cupid,
But kept their hearts with purpose stout
    For us 'gainst homeguards stupid.

TABLE OF CONTENTS.

	PAGE
Prelude	2
Dedication	3
The Campfire	7
Old Glory	10
Sam's Account of the Battle of Shiloh	12
The Freedmen	18
Logan at Atlanta	21
The Song on the Battlefield	26
The Soldier's Burial	28
Sinking of the Albemarle	29
Farragut at Mobile	31
Stampede of the Mule Brigade	33
Garfield's Ride	35
The Hospital Angel	37
In the Rifle Pits	39
The Girls We Left at Home	42
Winning a Star	44
Martyrs Fall—God's Cause Never	47
Allen Buckner	48
The Tale of a Drum	51
Buried	55
The Father's Quest	56
Grandpa Takes Selma Once More	60
Blow, Bugler, Blow	63
The Fatal Lot	64
The Brothers	70
Charge of Minty's Brigade	73
Will and Nellie	76
A Sentiment	80
A Tribute to My Wife	81
The Bugler	82
Dress by the Flag	84
The Veteran and the Flag	87
Fight It Out on This Line	92
One by One	95
Jim	97
The Gray's Last Campaign	101
The Drummer Boy's Dirge	102

CONTENTS.

All Quiet on the Potomac	103
Be Not Dismayed	105
The Compact of the Blue and the Gray	106
Charles Carroll of Carrollton	108
Cuba Libre	110
Blue-Coat Joe and Gray-Coat John	111
Peace	116
Hang Out Thy Light	121
Raising of Lazarus	123
Waiting For Jesus	132
Dot's Love-Letter	136
I Looked in Her Eyes	137
The Silver Anniversary	138
Ship, Ahoy!	141
The Meadow Lark	143
Into the Furnace	145
Lake Michigan	147
The Revolt in the Museum	155
Lend a Hand	158
Help Him When He's Down	160

Come gather, boys, the campfire round,
As we were wont to do.

THE CAMPFIRE.

Come gather, boys, the campfire round,
 As we were wont to do
Where, mid the siege gun's awful sound,
 The deadly missiles flew.
The chickens simmer in the pot,
 The pig is broiling brown;
We've hard tack tough as any knot,
 None tougher in the town.

Full rations here for every one,
 Enough and some to spare;
We'll fill each haversack with fun
 And tidbits rich and rare.
Here's hard tack toast and boiled beans too,
 And chicken fricasseed,
And ham and eggs and every new
 And racy dish you need.

No raiding Johnnies are about
 To tear the railroads up
Or put the wagon trains to rout
 And leave us not a sup.

No hunger pangs our stomachs feel,
    For want of bread and meat ;
Our grub no commissaries steal,
    While we half rations eat.

So gather round the campfire's blaze ;
    Yes, gather one and all ;
Those stirring scenes of other days
    Endeavor to recall.
Astonish friends and neighbors too
    With tales of valor great ;
Tell stories old and stories new ;—
    Let each one have its mate.

Unfurl the banner that we love,
    Her azure field behold.
Our fathers brought down from above
    The gems which deck each fold.
And, boys, we never lost one star,
    Though treason foulest tried
To tear a handful out and mar
    That flag, the patriot's pride.

Of saber charge let troopers tell,
    Of fearless, dashing raid,
And show us how they gave the yell
    That made the rebs afraid :
And then, how they sometimes turned tail
    And, in a steeple chase,
Went leaping brush and log and rail
    For rear at break-neck pace.

Let sailors too the tale unfold,
    As jolly tars well can,
The tale that often has been told,
    How Farragut once ran
The gauntlet hot on Mobile bay,
    How Foot Fort Henry took,
How Porter tread the fiery way
    And Vicksburg's power shook.

Let those who in the trenches lay
    'Fore Richmond, fortress-walled,
Or at Atlanta saw the day
    That lion hearts appalled,—
Let these cause every hair to rise,
    And straight on end to stand
With stories only he denies
    Who took with them no hand.

Our rifles hang upon the wall:
    Our sabers rusted are:
Our sons must answer to the call,
    Should call there be for war.
Let us today bring best good cheer;—
    Come, each your rations take;
Let wit and humor sparkle here
    And songs the echoes wake.

OLD GLORY.

Ay; call our loved banner "Old Glory,"
　　For thus it was christened in blood,
The blood of the nation's most loyal,
　　When perils swept in like a flood.
Where the smoke of the battle was densest,
　　And missiles of death hurtled by,
Above all the conflict and carnage,
　　The stars and the stripes floated high.

It is not the proud flag of a tyrant
　　Who crushes all freemen to earth;
It is not the base emblem of serfdom
　　That tells of an ignoble birth;
It is not the red anarchist's guidon,
　　That symbol of hate, crime and wrong;
'Tis the flag of Columbia's glory,
　　The theme of the patriot's song.

Each star on her azure blue union,
　　Each stripe, whether crimson or white,
Is a pledge to the far away pilgrim
　　Of help to maintain every right.

Raise high this proud ensign of freedom;
    Salute it with salvo and cheer;
For we love every fold of Old Glory,
    The one flag that despots all fear.

'Tis the flag of a free born people,
    Of a nation that knows not a slave,
Of a land the sworn foe to oppression,
    The home of the free and the brave.
Yes, call it Old Glory forever;
    Enshrine in our hearts every star
Of that banner that flutters so proudly,
    In peace, as aforetime in war.

It stands for so much to the nations
    Of promise for downtrodden man;
'Tis a beacon of hope to the hopeless,
    And all who are under the ban,
Where tyranny loads with its fetters,
    And cruelly places its heel
On the necks of the suffering millions,
    E'en while they as suppliants kneel.

Blow the bugle; assemble the veterans
    Who fought lest her stars become dim;
And rally their sons and their daughters
    To join in one jubilant hymn;
Bid the youth of the nation assemble,
    From Northland and Southland as well;
Raise all voices in praise of Old Glory,
    And ring a new Liberty Bell.

SAM'S ACCOUNT OF THE BATTLE OF SHILOH.

I tell you, boss, that Shiloh fight jest beat 'em all
 complete;
De Yanks got badly whipped befo' de rebels dey
 defeat.
Dis darkey he hab all de fun of fightin' dat he want,
When Johnson like a cyclone came a dashin' on to
 Grant.
I led a horse for Capen Snow that bloody day, ye see,
An' early in the mawnin', sah, de capen said to me,
Sez he, "Now, Sam, there's goin' to be a red hot time
 today,
"I feel it in my bones, my boy, the very ol' Nick's
 to pay;
"An', Sam' no matter what may come, your duty you
 must do,
"An' have my extra saddle horse, my Fanny, brave
 an' true,
"Where I can quickly mount again, if Charley 'neath
 me falls,
"Before the storm I'm sure will come, the storm of
 leaden balls."

Well, suah enough, there was a fight, a right smart
 peart one, too;
Twas awful, sah, de way dem shells an' canister dey
 flew.

De darkeys mos'ly keep de rear when fightin' has
    begun ;
But capen he might need dat horse, an' what would he
    hab done,
If Sam had put for de Tennessee when dem big cannon
    roared,
An' screechin' shells with sputterin' fuse amid de tree
    tops soared?
But I can tell you, Massa Jones, dis darkey wished
    dat day,
When dem big shells came sailin' in, dat he was miles
    away ;
For when dey busted 'mong the men dey made such
    awful soun',
Dey sent de shivers on my back go chasin' up an' down ;
My skin jes' crep' an' crawled an' twitched, my bref
    came quick an' fast,
I thought that every minute, sah, was sure to be my
    last.

Cap. Snow he fought wid Billy Sherman on de right
    out dar,
'Twas jest de place dat bullets flew, if dey flew any
    whar ;
An' when de Johnnies made a charge an' tried his line
    to bend,
It took de krinkles from my wool, an' made it stan'
    on end.
I tried to get behin' de hoss, to save my bacon, sah ;
For I'd agreed to sarve Cap. Snow clar through de
    civil wah,

An' what was any darkey wuth, when punctured like
 a sieve,
To sarve his massa at de mess, or help to him to give ?
An' then, sez I, "see here, you Sam, you bettah up
 an, dus',
"You ol' black coward, what you doin', makin' sech
 a fuss ?
"Suppose a ball should hit bay Fan, 'cos you behin'
 her stan'.
You ornary, sneakin', worthless cur; say, what you
 good for den ?"

So I jest mounted on my mule, an' turned bay Fan
 about,
When yondah came de Johnnies, sah, as though all
 hell was out.
De way dey yelled an' screeched dat day, sah, beat a
 savage Sioux ;
It made de tree tops sway an' ben' to let the racket
 frough ;
But den you ough' to see dem Yankees pile 'em up in
 heaps ;—
Dos' minnie balls do pow'ful wuk as through de
 ranks dey sweeps.—
I guess bay Fan was scared a bit to hear such mighty
 racket,
For first I know we's goin', sah, as fast as we could
 make it,
For Tennessee's swift flowin' stream whar dos' big
 gunboats lay :—
Wha's dat, you say, you nigga dar ? Dat "I was scared
 dat day?"

See here, you lyin', sneakin' trash, you bettah
 car'fu' be :
"Twas Fan got scairt, an' not ol' Sam, she ran away
 wid me.

Well, when we struck de Tennessee jest over nigh de
 bend,
Dat ol' big gunboat opened up, an' blazed from end
 to end.
Gee Whew! I thought de world had bust, an' judg-
 ment day had come,
When dem big cannon all went off an' hurled dar
 load of bomb ;
An' somethin', jest as sure's you live, clean knocked my
 head gear off,—
My krinkly ha'r had riz again, it had, sah, suah
 enough.
De way dem gunboats howled an' roared, dis darkey
 never heard,
Dey raised de mischief wid de rebels an' dar columns
 jest devoured.
Den all de Yankees an' de rebs got in an awful mix,
You couldn't tell de one from t'other, for dey both was
 cuttin' sticks ;
De rebels runnin' for de woods, de Yankees for de
 ribber,—
I tell you, sah, de way it went, it made dis darkey
 shibber.

An' den I said, "see here, you Sam, de Capen wants
 dis hoss :
" 'Cos ober dar whar he has fought dey suffered awful
 loss ;

"You bettah face dem cannon quick, that's mowin'
    down de men,
" An' start your boots an' go right smart, to find de
    Cap again."
So I jest shet my teeth so tight I cracked some three
    or four,
An' run dat hoss wid all my might back dar a mile
    or more.
De men was runnin' t'other way wid all dar might an
    main,
An' some dey grab at Fanny's head an' tried to grab
    de rein;
But I was arter Capen Snow, an' Fanny seemed to know;
She sent her heels at some ob dem, an' some she give
    a blow,
An' clean jumped ober some dar heads, an' den she
    dashed ahead,
Whar cannon ball flew thickly, sah, an' thicker flew
    de lead.

Dey howled about on ebery side; dey tore and plowed
    de groun'
Dey cut de branches from de trees, an' scattered dem
    aroun;
An' jest as Capen I espied, a limpin' long afoot,
Dar somethin' took an' lifted me, an' laid me cross
    a root;
I thought a shell had hit me, sah, an' busted 'gainst
    my head;
It made it feel as big's a squash an' like a ton o' lead;
An' when I gathered up myself, an' looked aroun' de
    field,

I couldn't tell which way was which; dis nigga's
 senses reeled.
But I can tell you, pretty soon I saw dem rebels goin'
Wid all dar might de odder way, while shells dar ranks
 was mowin'.
De Yankees too was lookin' blue, dar ranks were broke
 an' trying'
To beat de rebels runnin' way, an' each wid other
 vicin'.

When I foun' Capen Snow again, a week had gone
 away,
An' Capen thought dat I was killed on dat hot Shiloh
 day.
He said dat I had cracked my head against an' ol'
 oak limb,
While tryin' all my might, sah, ol' bay Fan to bring
 to him.
"De rebels thought dey had us, Sam, a day or two ago ;
"But, when dey foun' dat Sherman's boys could give
 dem blow for blow,
"Dey turned about an' run like mad, an' now are
 miles away ;
"I tell you, Sam, dey got enough on Shiloh's bloody day.
"Dey thought dey whip us pow'ful quick, an' gobble
 ebery one,
"When dey set up dat awful yell, an' fired dar ol'
 big gun ;
"But you bettah believe dey missed dar count, an' dey
 got awful sick,—
"Dey came quick time to Shiloh, Sam, dey left at
 double quick."

THE FREEDMEN.

      The day's work was over;
      And now, under cover,
      They gathered in quarters,
The cooks and the butlers, the cutters and carters;
      Full of glee,
            They felt free;
Till the morning the driver should bring to their door,
To compel them to shoulder their burdens once more.

      Such laughing and shouting;
      Now and then, too, some pouting,
      As some ebon Nancy
Imagined that Caesar had taken a fancy,
      Not due,
            To some Sue,
Whose face had bleached out to a butternut tan,
That gave her more beauty than ebony Nan.

      Jim Crow was now telling,
      With pathos most thrilling,
      How poor old Dan Tucker,
The slow, lazy coach one time lost all his supper;
      While Joe,
            Son of Crow,
With whooping hilarious and many a shakedown,
Was whirling and shuffling and dancing a breakdown.

      Such innocent folly,
      Where all were so jolly;

The corn shucking ended,
The banjos dull twang with the tambourine blended;
Then long
Swells of song
Rose and fell like the tide on the shores of the sea,
And the voices of slaves sang the songs of the free.

Mysterious Japhet,
The snowy-haired prophet,
To himself slowly mutters,
While the wind howling by shakes the cabin's loose shutters,
Till around
On the ground
They sit, and such hush settles down over all
That the tread of the cricket is heard on the wall.

"My chillen; oh, my chillen,
"De Lawd s ben revealin',
"In midnight's deep vision,
"Dat de time is mos' here, when de chain ob oppression
"Shall be broken
"In token
"Ob de glorious day when He come in de cloud
"To lift up de lowly an' abase all de proud.

"Dis way he is sweepin',
"His covenant keepin';
"My ears seem now hearin'
"De soun' ob his chariot; I know it is nearin'.
"He comes,
"Surely comes:
"Arouse, ye that slumber: each cabin prepare;
"Gib de Lawd de bes' room, when He comes in de air."

His voice then grew weaker,
Until ceased the speaker ;
And still they sat musing,
And silently thought, none the message refusing.
But a shout,
Loud and stout,
Woke the echoes again, filling all with amaze,
As Joe sprang among them, his eyes all ablaze.

"I'se sure dey is comin' :
"Bress de Lawd, dey is comin',
"De great Massa Linkum,
"Wid de sogers, I heard de great chariots clinkum ;
"An' dey say
"Dat today
"Dey'll be here about campin', an' bugle an' drum
"Will announce dat de jubilee surely hab come.

"Tell to all de sweet story ;
"Then to God be all glory,
"Who himself will e'er lead us,
"An' while in de wilderness, manna will feed us ;
"An' de ark,——
"But hark !
"Don' ye hear de great wheels ob de Lawd's chariot
rumble ?
"Oh, de powerful horse ob de Lawd nevah stumble."

Then the blues came in sight,
Marching on in their might ;
With a firm, fearless tread,
On they swept toward the sea with brave Sherman ahead.
Everywhere
On the air,

The proud ensign was floating, the red, white and blue,
Pledging freedom to all, and not to the few.

      How they shout, "Halelujah!"
      From the mountains of Beulah,
      They could see beyond Jordan :
"March quickly," they cry, "Ie's the ribber be fordin',
        "The blessin'
            "Possessin'."
But they saw not the giants, so tall and so fierce,
Or the strong fortress walls which their valor must pierce.

      Weary years they had waited,
      In thralldom they hated ;
      And, each banner caressing,
Their voices they raised in a paean of blessing.
      They clung,
          While they sung,
To the flag ; and they told, in their rapturous love,
Of their faith that God's angel would come from above.

LOGAN AT ATLANTA.

  Awake your lyre, my muse, and tell
In martial strains of what befel
    On that great day in sixty-four,
When 'neath Atlanta's frowning walls
Was heard the whistling minnie balls,
    And loud the cannon's awful roar.

Columbia then was in the throes
Of civil war with all its woes ;
    And blood in crimson rivers flowed
Where North and South, in strife arrayed,
Had each unsheathed the battle blade,
    To reap where treason rank had sowed.

That day, near hour of sultry noon,
While wood and dale were all in tune,
    And lovely bird sang sweetest strain,
All happy in their woodland haunt,
Where none superior right could vaunt,
    While nature joined in their refrain,
The Union troops with spirits fine
Were pressing on in marching line,
    Suspecting not a lurking foe ;
When all at once, with fearful yell,
They dashed upon them from the hill
    To crush McPherson at a blow.

Adown the hill, across the glen,
There rushed a multitude of men
    To fall like grass before the scythe :
Death rode there too in horrid mien,
A royal harvest here to glean,
    While dying scores about him writhe.
The Army of the Tennessee
Prepares to join the fierce melee,
    That overwhelming charge to check ;
So loud the roar and clash of arms,
It seemed as though a thousand storms
    Each drove a thousand ships to wreck.

Like ocean wave against the rock,
Which meets but to repel the shock,
    E'en so that surging wave of men
Are hurled against that solid wall,
And shattered, scattered, back they fall,
    To rally, cheer and charge again.
How the grape shots hissed ; how the bullets flew :
Making terrible gaps in their pathway through,
    And dyeing the sod with a crimson stain !
The rushing, roaring, rattling shells,
Hurled forth from the throats of blazing hells,
    Sped on their way through the mass of men.

They left behind their course a lane,
Filled with mangled, gory slain,
    To wash out treason's stain with blood.
Bullets and shells, with discordant scream,
O'er all did chant a hoarse requiem
    Which drove the songsters from the wood.
Amid that storm of awful grandeur
Still rode in front their loved commander,
    Where'er the air with death was rife.
Each danger sharing with the men,
A shining mark once and again,
    He fell at last bereft of life.

But who comes yonder riding fast,
His martial cloak from shoulder cast?
    'Tis Logan comes to save the day ;
His long black hair streams on the wind,
His staff are left far, far behind,
    So eager he to lead the fray.

"McPherson and revenge!" he cries,
As down the line he swiftly flies,
    And volleyed round on round reply;
The air seems full of shot and shell,
So fast they send them in and well,
    As each repeats that hoarse war-cry.

And now behold in great confusion,
The blue and gray, with fierce contusion,
    Falling, rising, fighting on;
Now steel meets steel in feint and thrust,
And trampling feet raise clouds of dust
    To help the smoke blot out the sun.
With eager, wild enthusiasm,
The foemen fill each yawning chasm,
    Where swept the grape and canister.
Each gap is closed without a pause,
E'en while within the very jaws
    Of death; closed up without a fear.

With flashing eye stands Logan there,
While deathshots hurtle through the air,
    And hurls defiance at the foe;
Unmoved amid that leaden hail,
Before which many stout hearts quail,
    He more than deals them blow for blow.
Loud roars the dread artillery,
Sharp sounds the rattling musketry,
    And checks them in their mad career.
There's a lull in the fight, while the wind lifts the
    smoke,

And discloses the assailants disordered and broke,
    While piles of the dead and the dying appear.

Yet nothing daunted by defeat,
Still on they come again to meet
    The awful storm which o'er them broke ;
All surging on tumultously,
While guns are belching rapidly,
    They plunge again into the smoke,
Then scale the hill and palisade,
And, hand to hand and blade to blade,
    They grapple and the conflict rages.
The folds of our banners and theirs intertwine,
So hotly it rages throughout the whole line,
    As rebel with patriot in battle engages.

The eagle eye of Logan notes
Where every banner proudly floats ;
    What perils black his corps assail.
Where deathshots thickest fall his shout
Inspires friend, puts foe to rout.
    Unmindful of the sleet and hail,
Blow answers blow ; steel crosses steel.
His heated cannon loudly peal,
    His men like heroes stand the shock,
Till, baffled and beaten back rolls the tide,
Rolls back o'er the streamlet with crimson dyed,
    As angry sea billows recoil from the rock.

THE SONG ON THE BATTLE-FIELD.

The great battle was o'er and the foemen, at rest
    On their arms, were awaiting the day,
To renew the hot fight where each other they pressed
    Or stood like the red deer at bay.
There was blood on the meadows, all trampled and torn;
    There was blood where the oak cast its shade ;
There were thousands who lay where they fell in the morn
    When the desperate onslaught was made.

From that terrible field rose the moanings of pain
    From the fallen who lay in their gore,
And fever parched lips prayed for water in vain,
    As their wounds became stiffened and sore.
Not a surgeon to dress or to wash the torn limb ;
    Not a comrade to bathe the hot brow ;
As the twilight's last ray slowly faded, till dim
    Bright Arcturus sent forth a faint glow.

Then afar on the right rose a tremulous song,
    Scarcely heard though the night was so still ;
And we listened amazed as it drifted along,
    While responsive each heart felt a thrill.
We wondered such sound from the red field to hear,
    A song on the verge of despair,
And we listened in awe, then each one dropped a tear,
    As we thought of the sufferer there.

"We'll rally around the old flag, my boys,
    Yes we'll rally there once again."
Still louder and louder arose the sweet voice,
    Till the singer grew weaker, and then
It as slowly died out as the life ebbed away,
    And the heart felt the cold deathly chill ;
Then a hush like the grave held the blue and the gray,
    As the song and the singer were still.

But another took up the glad chorus unsung,
    And still others joined in the refrain,
Till a volume of song o'er the battle-field hung,
    While the wounded forgot the mad pain :
"The union forever, hurrah ! boys, hurrah !"
    The slumbering echoes awoke ;
"Then down with the traitors and up with the stars,"
    Like a volley o'er battle-field broke.

A thousand parched lips, with a quiver of pain,
    Caught the sweet inspiration of song,
Though the fountain of life felt the terrible drain,
    And stiff was the fever parched tongue.
'Twas a baptismal hymn for the flag of the free,
    Round the font with their blood running o'er,
And, forgetting the wounds, each one sang it in glee,
    As no voices e'er sang it before.

THE SOLDIER'S BURIAL.

Dead on the picket line,
Down where the whispering pine
Sings o'er his body a mournful requiem ;
Pierced by a musket ball,
Where no one saw him fall,—
Sleeping the sleep ne'er disturbed by a dream.

Tenderly comrades true
Gather to bid adieu,
Dropping a tear o'er the soldier that's dead.
They may tomorrow lie
Under the burning sky,
Bleeding and dying where his blood was shed.

Muffle the drum and subdue the shrill fife ;
Hush every voice as we turn from the strife ;
Gather in sadness about the lone bier ;
Weep for the comrade now slumbering here.
Soft tread the steps while we bear to his grave,
Where Chattahoochie his feet may e'er lave,
This our loved comrade and lay him away,
Safely to sleep till the last judgment day.
Disturb not his rest as he sleeps 'neath the sod,
Here where in vigor of manhood he trod ;
Fire a volley, the soldier's last token,
While o'er his grave our last farewells are spoken.

Beat the long roll for him
Softly, while twilight dim
Whispers the warrior its kindly good night ;
When the last trumpet sound
Echoes the world around,
This our dead comrade shall wake with the light.

SINKING OF THE ALBEMARLE.

What craft do we see stealing silently on
   Through the darkness and gloom of the night,
While the twinkle of campfires hither and yon
   Send out a faint glimmer of light?
With scarcely a puff of escaping steam,
She pushes her way 'gainst the onflowing stream.

She is nearing the wharf where the great Albemarle
   The water's calm bosom rides,
While the river's strong current, with soft, gentle purl
   Laves the vessel's dark iron sides.
A tiny launch is the moving boat,
The ironclad dark is a fortress afloat.

A sudden hail from the watch on her deck,
   A blazing of lights from the shore,

And the foe is awake to avert the wreck,
    And her wrath on the launch to pour.
A flash and a thunder that shook all the hills,
And the blood stains the deck of the launch in red rills.

But Cushing is not of the spirit that quails
    When perils fast thicken around ;
His not the faint heart that ignobly fails,
    And hastens its weapons to ground,
When the foe is aroused and comes forth from his lair,
And the hot iron hail whistles shrill through the air.

The cylinders groan with the pressure of steam,
    And the launch swiftly dashes in
'Gainst the log barricades that are floating abeam,
    Unminding the cannon's loud din.
For 'tis better to sink 'neath the turbulent wave,
Than to fail of one's duty and life to save.

From the topmost deck to the water's edge
    The engines of death are blazing;
But the launch plows on midst the logs and the sedge,
    Till the sides of the vessels are grazing.
Never blanches a face in the furnace of fire,
But each scornfully laughs at the enemy's ire.

Upheaved from their bed the dun waters arise,
    While the ironclad shivers and groans ;
Then prone on the bottom the huge kraken lies,
    And o'er her the cold water moans.
She has done her last work, she lies low in her grave,
For the vigilant watchmen were helpless to save.

Tell the story again ; let the sons oft repeat
    How their sires destruction once dared ;
How they fearlessly sailed, how they brooked no defeat,
    How their breasts to the hailstorm they bared.
Bid them hang on the tomb of the fallen a wreath,
And honor the flag that their fathers bequeath.

FARRAGUT AT MOBILE.

Round shot, and chain shot, with hot shot and shell,
Vomited forth from the throat of that hell,
When the ship Hartford steamed up the long bay,
Leading the van in the heat of the fray.
Strong is the swell of the waves 'neath her keel ;
Thunderous broadsides and quick make her reel ;
Morgan and Gaines both are sulphurous mines,
Hurling destruction at Farragut's lines,
Pounding the ribs of each ship of the fleet,
Sweeping their decks with a hot iron sleet.

Up in the top the brave admiral stands,
Lashed to the mainmast with glass in his hand,
Guiding the fleet on its perilous way
Into the furnace where victory lay ;
Each open port is with fire ablaze,
While he is steadily treading the maze,
Where with torpedo and gunboat and chain,
Mobile was sure he would seek it in vain.
How the ship shivers beneath the recoil,
Now that each gunner is into the broil !

Down go the ironclads floating the bars,
Sunk by the broadsides of Farragut's tars.
Thus the old war-dogs, ablaze fore and aft,
Sweeping the bay of its traitorous craft,
Dash through the waves while so thickly and fast
Shells tear their bulwarks or fly screaming past,
Staining the decks of a dark crimson dye,
Cutting the rigging above them on high,
Rending each hull as they burst 'gainst its side,
Scattering fragments about far and wide.

Sturdy old rovers, those seamen who sail,
Following on in the Hartford's hot trail ;
Bronzed are their faces with tropical sun,
Blackened with smoke as each stands to his gun,
Sending his challenge to each rebel fort,
Jesting in danger as though it were sport,
Cheering in glee as each shot found its targe,
Springing to place and renewing the charge.
Morgan and Gaines, to their infinite grief,
Find their dominion is fleeting and brief.

Past the great forts and the bars have come down,
While in their stead the broad stripes are outthrown,
Greeting the breezes that sighed for so long
For the old banner, the patriot's song ;
Proudly the waters sweep on toward the sea,
Greeting once more the dear flag of the free,
Fondling the ships with a tender caress,
Touching each prow with a lover's fond kiss.
On toward the city sweeps the jubilant fleet,
Eager the foe in his stronghold to meet.

STAMPEDE OF THE MULE BRIGADE.

Decatur, near Atlanta, 1864.

Bang ! 'Twas a carbine the echoes awaking,—
Guard of the packtrain now slumbering near.
Bang ! Rattle, bang ! The still night's quiet breaking,
Gun answering gun, and cheer to each cheer.
    Drivers go hurrying,
    Everywhere skurrying,
    Oh, what a flurrying !
Faces once black are now ashen with fear.

Saddles and packs on the mules each one throwing,
Mounts in hot haste and then dashes away,
Each sable rider assuredly knowing
Where there were guns there was mischief to pay.
    Angry shouts ringing,
    Minnie balls winging,
    Each shrilly singing,
Tells that the pickets are into the fray.

Frantic the efforts the darkeys are making,
Each with his packmule to lead in the race ;
Palsied with terror, his body is quaking,
While 'neath the spur his mule quickens his pace.
    Frying pans pounding,
    Kettles resounding,
    As they go bounding,
Each at his best in a wild steeple chase.

Full of the spirit of self preservation,
Darkeys and donkeys flew down through the corn,
Laying it low with a swift devastation,
Leaving the cornfield all trampled and torn.
    Arms wildly swinging,
    Campkettles ringing,
    Scared riders clinging,—
O what a sight at the first streak of morn!

On they all go in a desperate scramble,
Riding for life, and each doing his best,
Over the fences and down through the bramble,
Hearts wildly beating in each sable breast.
    What a skedaddle!
    Every packsaddle
    All in a muddle!
Rolling and tumbling but never at rest.

Paul Revere's ride was a wonderful story,
Winning for him an undying fame;
Sheridan rode to a field that was gory,
Making immortal the general's name;
    But for a slashing,
    Time record smashing,
    Ride that was dashing,
Both Phil's and Paul's were decidedly tame.

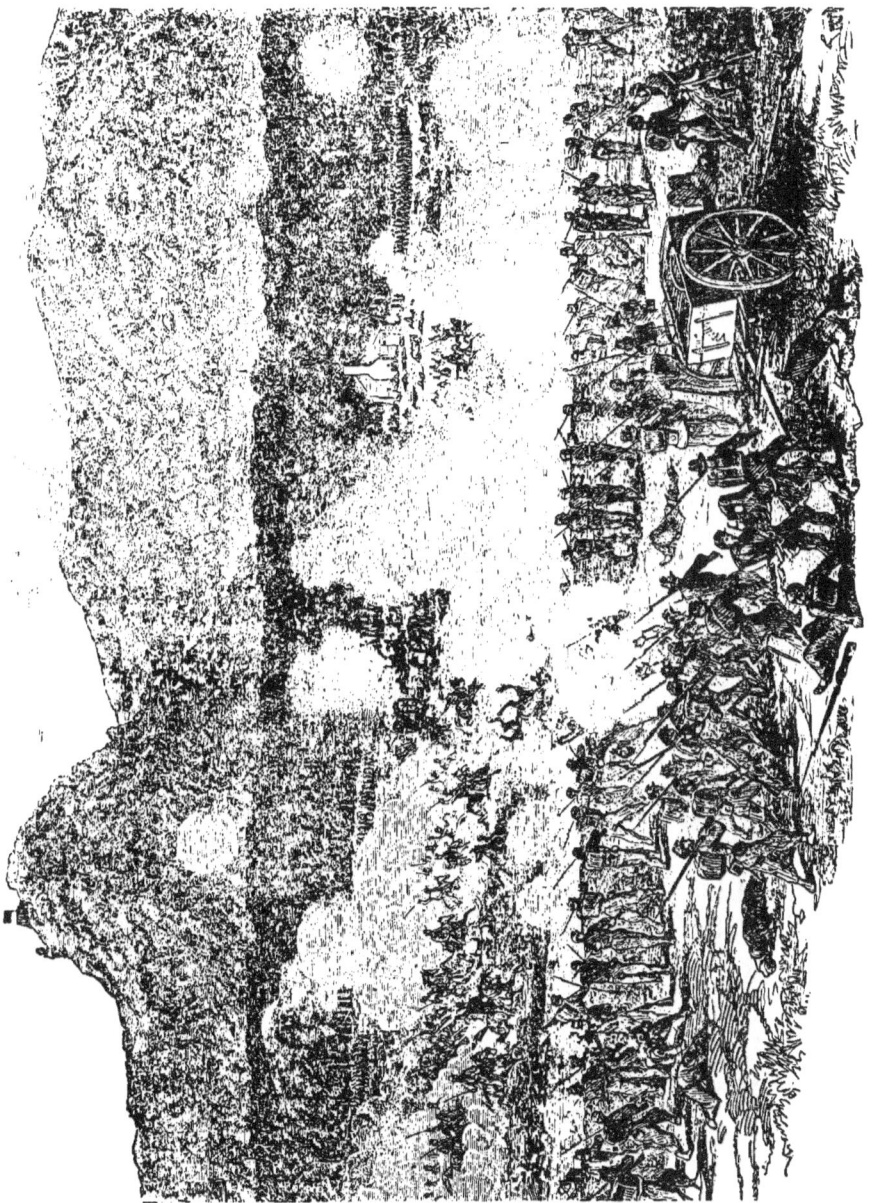

Thomas was bleeding at every pore,
Stemming the tide the red field rolling o'er.

GARFIELD'S RIDE.

See yon bold horseman swift galloping on,
Hurling the pebbles both hither and yon,
Through the thick forest and tangled morass,
Each one defying the bravest to pass,
Leaping the fences and climbing each hill,
Heart all aglow and soul in a thrill:
Garfield the man, name we cherish and love,
He for whom fame has the bay leaf enwove.

Thomas was bleeding at every pore,
Stemming the tide the red field rolling o'er,
Firm as a rock on the storm-beaten coast,
Hurling to death the fierce on-rushing host.
Hopeless the day if the Rock were o'erthrown;
Whelmed was an army, its sun had gone down.
See on his flank foemen jubilant press;
See in the rear yonder threatening mass.

On like the wind speeds the foamy flecked steed,
Urged by the rider, increasing his speed;
Mile after mile he still stretches away,
Till from the front come the sounds of the fray.
Rolling artillery thunders afar;
Sputtering shells scream everywhere;
Louder, still louder, the horrible din,—
Which one is losing, and which one shall win?

This is the query that troubles the one
Spurring his horse and still urging him on :
What if too late comes the message he brings !
Maddening thought ! To his speed it lends wings.
Deeper the rowels sink into the side ;
Wilder the steed plunges o'er the divide,
Faithfully striving his duty to do,
Straining each nerve for his rider so true.

"Halt!" from the wood comes the urgent command.
"Halt or you die !" and before him there stand
Scores of armed foemen to block up the path,
Armed to the teeth and each breathing out wrath.
Quickly he wheels ; to his horse he gives rein :
Over the fence and then onward again.
Oh what a roar ! How the minnie balls flew,
Cutting the air and his uniform too !

Once and again hear the volleys belch forth,
Trying his mettle and testing his worth.
Down? Yes, his horse has been stricken at last,
Pinning him down and then holding him fast :
No, he is off like a fleet-footed deer ;
Bullets still fly, but he laughs at all fear.
Horses may fall and his rider may die,
Garfield the hero will duty ne'er fly.

Horsemen are coming ; he points to the foe,
Vaults to a saddle still onward to go,
Hastens where Thomas stands firm as a rock,
Warns him of danger ; he arms for the shock :

Foemen exulting dash in on the run ;
Met, they are broken and victory won.
Who can forget the brave Garfield's great ride,
Thomas to save and a battle decide?

THE HOSPITAL ANGEL.

Lovingly dedicated to my mother, Ruth E. Whitwam, now nearly eighty-four years old, who gave three sons to maintain the honor of the flag, two of them mere boys, all that she had old enough. She herself then went to the front in '64, and on the battlefield of Columbia, Tenn., amid the crashing shot and shell, helped to take care of the wounded as they were brought and laid beside her all torn and bleeding. In the hospitals at Columbia, Nashville and Louisville, while nursing her youngest soldier boy back to life, she became an angel of mercy to scores of other boys who lay suffering and dying, and their fervent ' God bless you's" have followed her all these years. God bless that soldier mother.

She came not on snowy white pinions ;
   She wore not a pearly white robe ;
No stars shone among her dark tresses ;
   She was not from the heavenly abode.
No halo shed glory about her,
   Like that about canonized saint :—
She was only a mortal, a woman,
   An heir to the Edenic taint.

But love-hungry eyes watched her moving,
   A smiling, sweet angel of love,
Through the wards where the men who were dying,
   Needed some one to point them above :

Where the wounded lay helpless and hopeless,
  She brought them a brave word of cheer;
Where in agonized pain they were tossing,
  Her sympathy lent them a tear.

On a cot near the door was one dying;
  A grape-shot had shattered his limb;
She sat, at his wish, by the bedside,
  And softly she sang a sweet hymn;
His mother's dear voice used to sing it,
  When, a child, he had stood at her knee;
With a smile he the precious name murmured,
  And his soul from the body was free.

The quinine e'en tasted less bitter,
  When she by the patient would stand;
The pillows were softer and fresher,
  Shaken out by her own lily hand;
The toast looked so nice and inviting,
  The coffee as clear as could be,
When, with face all a-cheery and smiling,
  She sat with the tray on her knee.

She talked of their wives and their sweethearts,—
  Each one his full confidence gave—
And many a sweet, loving message
  Her pen hastened northward, to save
Bitter tears to the anxious ones waiting
  For tidings, that else had scarce come,
Of the loved ones who fell by the banner,
  And suffering lay far from home.

Many voices were raised to the Father
    Which had never addressed Him before,
Asking Him to pour blessings upon her,
    The richest of heaven's rich store;
I am sure the petitions were answered,
    For brighter she grew with each day,
Shedding beams of the heavenly glory
    On each pillow where sufferers lay.

We are dreaming today of that angel,
    Though thirty long years have gone by,
Since she came to the wards, as we fancied,
    Straight down from her home in the sky:
And we know that in one of those mansions
    The Saviour went up to prepare,
That sweet human angel will welcome
    The soldiers who call on her there.

IN THE RIFLE-PITS.

"Say, Jim, this looks pokish-like—lucky it's dark;
By daylight we'd make 'em an elegant mark.
Let us pile a few rails just along by this tree,
An' lay 'em down easy an' soft for, ye see,
The Johnnies are watchin'—I thought so; look out!
That shot took a button slick off o' my coat.
Hold on! I'll return his polite salutation,—
We Yanks draw good manners with every ration.
There now; let's lie low, while we scoop out a hole
An' roll up the dirt like a gopher or mole.

"Hullo! there's another; that fellow loads quick;
An' he shoots pesky careless; that made a small nick
In the top o' my ear, an' a lock o' my hair
Went along with the bullet, cut clean off just there.
Let us make it so warm he will keep out o' sight,
An' quit burnin' his powder to stir up a fight.
Good! once more let him have it; keep sendin' 'em in;
We can make it quite lively when once we begin.
But hold! let me hail the fire eater an' see
If he's learned to be civil or if he can be.

"Hullo, there, you reb! have you got any 'backer?"
"You bet! a right smart, an' I'll trade for a cracker."
A plug for a hard tack, unsight and unseen,
Was hurled back and forth o'er the mediate green;
And while they bombarded each other this way,
Not a shot was e'er fired by blue or by gray.
"That's all, Mister Reb, tumble into your hole,
An' do it right quick, if you value your soul."
Then down each one plunged, and in less than a minute
The fight was renewed and all hands were in it.

Ping! "Hey! Duck your head, Jim, that came pretty close;
An inch to the right, 'twould have taken your nose.
Look out for the next,—there it comes; down you go;
I saw where the smoke puffed out yonder,—Hullo!
You blasted old rebel, I'll pay you for that;
It has put a nice hole through the crown of may hat.
You watch the big tree yonder, Jim, while I draw
A bead on the rascal and puncture his jaw."
Crack! "How do you like it, you dirty spalpeen?
Rats! my bullet just split on his lean bony chin."

Then crack go the rifles from every pit ;
"A groan ? Yes, Joe's dead and Charley hard hit."
The bullets speed by with a serpent's mad hiss,
Or tickle our cheeks with a fiery kiss.
"Lay low, every one ; let each hand, too, be steady ;
We don't know what's coming, but hold yourselves ready.
If the men with those popguns intend to come out,
Just show them that Uncle Sam's boys are about ;
And keep burnin' powder, it's not very dear ;
It will give them assurance that we are still here.

"The furies ! what's up ?   Guess an earthquake went by;
How it scattered the dirt, how the timbers did fly !
No ; 'twas just a twelve pounder that covered us up ;—
The fiends take that gunner, the mean dirty pup ;
Just give me a crack at the son of the south ;
He'll laugh from the salt water side of his mouth.
But what's come o' Jim ?   Bet he's run for the woods,
An' gobbled my knapsack an' all o' my goods ;
No ; what ! is that you, Jim, crawlin' out o' the ruin,
With your eyes both in mournin', mouth spittin' an'
    spuin' ?"

But the sun brings the battle line, flags proudly
    streaming,
The breastplates all burnished and bayonets gleaming ;
The pickets must lead, as they go for the works,—
Pile hot maledictions on craven who shirks.
Crack go the rifles, as forward we spring ;—
The Johnnies are lively ; their minnie balls sing.
We, too, are all doing the best that we can,
Dashing into their rifle-pits every man.

"Get out o' there, mister, we want them oursel',
Throw down that ol' musket, an' swallow that yell.

"I'll take of that 'backer another big slab ;
Just wholesale the lot, an' none o' your blab ;
But say, I'm no hog, here's a haversack full
Of bullet proof hard tack ; an' now ye best pull
For our rear double quick, for it's gettin' too hot,
Les' you want your ol' hull to be riddled with shot.
But hold on ; just to skim all the cream of the joke,
Guess I'll wind that ol' gun o' yours round this small oak.
Now git ! Say, hold on reb, I'll go along to ;
Let me lean on your shoulder ; my leg is bored through."

THE GIRLS WE LEFT AT HOME.

And here's to the girls we left at home,
    With chains of love they bind us,
And true to them in the days to come,
    Each one will surely find us ;
We'll stand by them as they by us stood,
    While we the rebs were fighting ;
They did the very best they could
    While prayers to God inditing.

They plowed the corn, they milked the cows,
    Throughout that time so olden ;
They stored the clover in the mows ;
    They reaped the harvest golden ;

They picked the lint with might and main,
    Our wounds to help in healing,
The while their hearts were filled with pain,
    And all their senses reeling.

They belted swords upon our thighs,
    Their lily fingers shaking,
We read the lovelight in their eyes,
    Although their hearts were breaking.
And still from duty none e'er lag,
    But with a faith most royal,
They teach our boys to love the flag
    To which their sires were loyal.

They stood by us in the days of yore,
    Those girls with silken tresses,
Though the home-guards sought them o'er and o'er,
    And pined for their caresses ;
And now their hair has turned to gray,
    Our cranky ways enduring,
We'll love them better every day,
    With knightly truth assuring.

Come on, my boys, once more fall in,
    Shake out the folds of "Old Glory",
Give three times three with a tiger in,
    And big base drum galore,
For every one, God bless them all,
    They cheer the way before us,
Each merry laugh is a fairy's call,
    Come all join in the chorus.

WINNING A STAR.

A captain stood before his tent,
    Sharp scanning the hill's incline,
Where puffs of smoke from the rifle-pits
    Betrayed the foeman's line.
A sluggish stream before him lay,
    Beyond, a tangled wood,
With hidden perils lurking there,
    Besetting every rood.

And these the thoughts now uppermost
    In this true patriot's breast :—
"I love my country, hate her foes,
    By whom she is now distressed ;
And much I yearn for wider field
    Of action in the war.
If faithful service counts for aught,
    I soon shall win a star."

E'en while his thoughts thus vaulted high,
    His general drew nigh,
And, "Custer," said the officer,
    "I wish that you would try
To bring me word from yonder brake,
    What force lie there concealed,
That I may plan for their surprise,
    And drive them from the field."

Young Custer's uniform was new,
    The stream was dark and dank ;
But in he plunged upon his quest,
    And reached the other bank.
At risk of life he quickly learned
    What he was sent to learn,
And then, with duty fully done,
    He hastened to return.

And thus, whene'er the trial came,
    Though dangers dark appalled,
Brave Custer never shirked his post,
    But went where duty called.
And, as the months and years went by,
    His fame spread wide and far,
Until, found faithful everywhere,
    He won and wore his star.

And thus, on life's great battle-fields,
    Amidst its busy strife,
Are honors for the faithful one
    Who dedicates his life
To earnest work for God and Right,
    For Home and Native Land,
And duty does, whate'er it be,
    And goes at God's command.

But think not honors you shall win,
    If, humble work despised,
You look and long for something great,
    For your own sake devised.

God ne'er entrusts to any man
    To lead his martial host,
Until, through humbler discipline,
    He fits him for the post.

The way to honor's lofty shrine
    By none is ever trod
Who scorns to do the duties small
    Which meet him on the road.
Each step is marked by service true,
    Perhaps with none to know;
But God, who never fails to see,
    Will blessings rich bestow.

Wouldst thou, then, angel plaudits win?
    Wouldst thou wear starry crown?
Take up thy cross, though, humble, it
    Seems not to pledge renown.
If thou canst not a leader be,
    To shout the column on,
Perhaps a stretcher thou canst bear,
    To save the wounded one.

A drop of water thou mayst bring
    To cheer some wounded soul,
Borne down beneath the load which grief
    Doth on his spirit roll;
Some word of cheer, a tender prayer,
    A friendly grasp of hand,
A smile, a tear, may burdens lift,
    And these can all command.

Go, seek for work of humblest kind ;
   Ask God's own hand to lead ;
For naught is small which God requires,
   But honor brings indeed.
To those who faithful prove at last,
   And serve throughout the war,
He gives a crown of glory bright,
   Full-gemmed with many a star.

MARTYRS FALL—GOD'S CAUSE NEVER.

In the heat of the strife, when the cause needs him most,
The leader has fallen, struck down at his post ;
   But the All-ruling Lord,
   Ever true to his word,
   Saves the cause of the right,
   By omnipotent might,
And sends a new captain to marshal the host.

Though the blood of God's heroes enrich every soil,
Where they fall by the scores in the midst of the broil ;
   Though humanity's weal
   Lie beneath the foe's heel.
   Truth never can die,
   Though it wounded may lie ;
God will cherish and care for the fruit of his toil.

When McPherson, struck low, from his saddle had reeled,
Faint hearts feared that his veteran army must yield ;

But a Logan was there,
His own bosom to bare,
And the onrushing foe
Was soon struck such a blow
That its columns recoiled and then fled from the field.

The Lovejoys and Haddocks may fall one by one,
E'er the work that they champion is fully begun ;
But the cause still moves on,
And the crown shall be won,
And the enemy's rout
Be announced with a shout,
In some day by and by, when the battle is done.

Ne'er despair then, my brother, though close by your side
Many heroes have fallen and martyrs have died.
On their graves place a wreath,
Where they sleep on the heath ;
Then, with faith in God's word,
Once again draw the sword,
And be not dismayed for the cause shall abide.

ALLEN BUCKNER.

A bent old veteran stood on the floor
Of his conference answering the roll call once more,
As the bishop his name had repeated.
The warm flush of youth had forevermore fled ;
The snows of the winters lay white on his head ;
But his brethren he cordially greeted.

'Twas a day that tried souls, that dark, terrible day
When Sherman's brave troops dashed into the fray.

Allen Buckner had come just to answer again,
When his name should be called with the army of men
   Who were heralds of Christ's great salvation.
In a voice that was broken he feebly replied,
Though exulting in Christ the Redeemer who died
   To redeem from their sins every nation.

Then another outspoke in his patriot zeal,
In a voice that rang forth like the trumpet's loud peal,
   Every bosom responsively stirring;
"Bishop, there stands the man who the column once led,
Charging up Mission Ridge, for he rode at the head,
   Mid the shot and the shell's awful whirring."

Quickly came the reply, "Colonel, give me your hand,
You deserve well the plaudits of all this good land,
   There are memories round your deeds clinging."
What a cyclone of feeling swept through the vast throng,
As their voices outpoured in a patriot song,
   That set all the arches aringing.

They remembered the day when his strong voice rang out
At the head of the column with jubilant shout,
   As they swept Mission Ridge of the foemen;
How the canopied smoke hung so low over all,
And along the red slope they saw thousands fall
   Of America's noblest born yoemen.

'Twas a day that tried soul s, that dark, terrible day
When Sherman's brave troops dashed into the fray

And climbed up the ridge's steep side,
While the cannon belched forth the red simoon of death,
And withered the columns with fiery breath,
  As the grape swept the hills far and wide.

All hail to the hero who rode in the van,
It needed a hero, it called for a man ;
  It was no dress parade they were facing.
Allen Buckner stood forth as a man for the hour,
Who in that awful day from no duty would cower,
  Who would shrink not, though death were menacing.

Up the storm furrowed hillside he fearlessly led,
While the emerald carpet turned speedily red,
  With the blood of the heroes fast falling ;
For the line was soon met by the canister shot,
Hurled forth from the cannon's mouth blazing and hot,
  And a sweep through the ranks that was galling.

Yet no one e'er faltered, not one e'er turned back,
Though the smoke of the battle grew denser and black,
  While above them the cannon were roaring ;
To the top of the ridge with a shout they on pressed,
And soon swept every foe from the hill's highest crest,
  And their broadsides into them were pouring.

Those were days long ago, yet their memory thrills,
And each patriot bosom exultantly swells,
  As we hail the old hero so hoary.
Twice a veteran now, crowned with honors he stands ;
Yet, though wounded and sore, though palsied his hands,
  He has won the full meed of his glory.

THE TALE OF A DRUM.

A camp within a lovely grove,
Its snow white tents of canvas wove,
Lay nestling in a southern vale,
Near by the Chattahoochie's trail.
The sun had reached the quartermark
Between the sunrise and the dark,
When forth there marched two drummers bold,
Their helmets bright as burnished gold.

Alone they sought a quiet dell,
A place remote, where music's spell
Might woven be with none to say,
"Away, thou noisy fiend, away!"
And now begins the horrid din.
The way they banged those drums was sin.
The snare drum clatters like a loom,
While loud the base sounds, boom on boom.

The birds in fright dart through the air,
The fox runs swiftly to his lair;
The very leaves are shivering, too,
And rattling off the morning dew.
But louder still becomes the crash;
Those drums must surely go to smash,
Unless a hostile musket shot
Comes echoing from some distant spot.

The rocks resound and hurl it back,
Until the echoes all distract;
It sounds as though all bedlam's out,
Or forty thousand fiends about.
But hold, what sees the big base drummer,
This startled, stalwart, Sherman's bummer?
'Tis surely something, tell me what—
Or has he heard a rebel shot?

His drumstick halts aloft in air ;
His eyes are fixed in steady stare ;
Then speaks he : "Say, by my red wig,
I pledge my word I see a pig.
O, wondrous magic of a name!
To paint the scene all words are tame.
At once each drum has ceased its thunder
As though its head were burst asunder.

So quiet now the noonday air,
The fox steals forth from out his lair ;
The squirrel scampers up the trees ;
And songs of birds ride on the breeze.
All nature wakes again in glee ;
And e'en the hum of busy bee
Is heard, as, darting mid the flowers,
He culls the sweets from Nature's bowers.

Then, creeping on the unconscious game,
That royal boar of classic fame,
They soon appear before his sight
And give that rebel pig a fright.

The combat deepens. "On, ye drummers!
Charge home the game ye fearless bummers;
'Twere shame, a burning shame, to see
That pig escape so audaciously."

Through tangled vines they press their way,
Intent to bring the game to bay,
While mocking bird, with whistle shrill,
Cheers on the race with loudest trill.
Soon charging forth on safety bent,
While they still strive to keep him pent,
The drummer falls the pig astride,
Compelled to take unwilling ride.

And such a ride none ever knew,
As that he took. They fairly flew
Along the bank where canebrake stood,
High waving o'er the river's flood.
His drum went bounding up and down,
Resounding all the hills around;
For every cane laid on a stroke,
That did a noisy imp invoke.

What bummer e'er had such a steed,
Or made a charge at such a speed!
With face to rear he blindly rode,
While hard in chase the other strode.
At last—O, why must I relate
That bummers e'er met such a fate—
The pig fell floundering from the bank,
And both beneath the waters sank.

The pig is dead. "And now," quoth one,
"Our task is only just begun ;
For orders strict on us are laid,
'Gainst soldiers making private raid."
Then spake the big bass drummer out,
"Why, don't you see, you silly lout ?
We'll hide the pig within my drum,
And cheat the colonel, surely, chum."

Thus on they went in solemn file,
With careless step that showed no guile ;
And ne'er a preacher looked more prim,
While humming o'er a pious hymn.
The sun is hastening out of sight,
As though old Phoebus had a fright ;
While, slowly filing down the glade,
The camp comes out for dress parade.

The band its place on right of line
Have taken, and their helmets shine ;
Then rings aloud the colonel's call
In tones that doth each one appall :
"What means this absence from your place ?
Your helmets bright yon band should grace ;
At double quick yourselves bestir,
And take your place without demur."

Alas ! what could that drummer do,
That drummer bold, that drummer true ?
Should he attempt to fill his place,
The day would bring him dark disgrace.

He whispers in the colonel's ear,
So low that none beside may hear,
"My drum, dear sir, is out of rig,
It holds between its heads a pig."

Then out that brave old colonel spoke,
And softly now the silence broke,
"I'm sorry, sir, to know you're sick,
But go to bed at double quick.
And say," he added, soft and low,
That none beside might ever know,
"When you unmuffle that big drum,
Be sure to send the colonel some."

BURIED.

Buried the strife that once harnessed as foemen
    Section 'gainst section in hostile array,
Each one forgetting the ties that should bind them,
    Each man determined his brother to slay ;
Buried so deep it defies resurrection,
    When it was done it was buried for aye;
Cursed be the traitor of Southland or Northland
    Now would make foes of the Blue and the Gray.

Blue and Gray dug its sepulchre deeply,
    Sealed with their blood the strong door of its tomb;
Gray, though unwittingly, wrought no less surely ;
    Both did their work mid the cannon's dull boom.

Each sought a different end to accomplish,
  Fighting the other, and each did his best,
Staking their all on the issue of battle ;
  When it was ended, the Gray acquiesced.

Roll Alleghany above the dead issue,
  Lest some base hand may yet drag it to light ;
Pile too the Cumberland higher and higher,
  Hide it for aye in the regions of night.
Blue and the Gray fought it out with the musket,
  Then each erased every sign of the strife,
Sheathed his good sword and returned to his fireside,
  Sworn to defend the old flag with his life.

Come ye who fought in the forefront of battle,
  Daring the worst as ye stood face to face,
Grasp each the hand of the other in friendship,
  Ne'er more to hatred or strife give a place.
Shoulder to shoulder march under Old Glory,
  Emblem of freedom throughout the broad world ;
Borne by the Blue and the Gray in the future,
  Let the old flag to each breeze be unfurled.

THE FATHER'S QUEST.

Far away from the field where the issue was tried,
  A father and mother were spending their days ;
At their country's first call there had gone from their side
To the front, their brave boy, their chief joy and pride,
  John, so faithful and loving in all of his ways ;

Where Picket had charged, and had then charged again,
Where were offered the greatest libations of blood.

And he was at Gettysburg, this they well knew,
But where was he now, their dear loved one so true.

The papers were searched, but no word could they find,
    Whether wounded or dead, or if left on the field ;
Only "missing"—how much in that word was combined !
What a picture of horrors it brought to the mind !
    What fancies of evil were by it revealed !
Till the father's deep love sent him forth on his quest,
To find and to fold his dear boy to his breast.

Over mountains he trod, until, footsore and lame,
    On the field torn and furrowed by battle he stood,
That red field where the foe had staked all in the game,
And lost and went back to the lair whence he came,
    Leaving Gettysburg's soil darker yet with his blood,
Where, mid the fierce storm and artillery roar,
Columbia richest libations did pour.

O'er the fresh trampled meadows he wearily trod,
    Where the wild surging lines had so angrily met,
With his eyes quickly scanning each foot of the sod,
And his heart raised in earnest entreaty to God ;
    He shouted, his soul on the search fully set,
In accents assuring, as louder they grew,
"John Warren, your father is looking for you."

Where Picket had charged, and had then charged again,
    Where were offered the greatest libations of blood,
Where like granite rock had stood Hancock's brave men,
Driving back the bold lion to innermost den,
    He walked and he ran, then halting he stood,

And his voice on the wings of the winds ever flew,
"John Warren, your father is looking for you.'

'Twas the cry of a father, the voice of the love
   Which e'er burns on the loyal hearts holiest shrine ;
That love which immortal came down from above
To follow the loved ones wherever they rove ;
   A love whose bright luster naught else can outshine.
Still louder he shouts, to his purpose still true,
"John Warren, your father is looking for you.

He saw, but he recked not the signs of the strife,
   How the shot and the shell the great tree trunks
      had torn ;
He heard in the distance the drum and the fife ;
But he sought for the "missing," more precious than
      life ;
   He thought not of rest; but though weary and
      worn,
Still re-echoed his challenge with energy new,
"John Warren, your father is looking for you."

In the depths of the forest two soldier boys lay,
   Where they sank when the swift flying shrapnel and
      shell
Reaped their harvest of blood on that terrible day,
When the Blue in a death grapple met the brave Gray.
   In pain and despair each one lay where he fell,
When a shout pierced the copsewood which one of them
      knew,
"John Warren, your father is looking for you."

"Quick, comrade," he said, "for I am too weak,
'Tis my father's dear voice, loudly calling his boy;
Can you answer his hail? O, hasten to speak;
Let him know he is here he is coming to seek.
It will bring to my father's great heart such a joy."
Then his comrade cried out till his blood flowed anew,
"John Warren your boy lies here waiting for you."

He bathed their hot brows and each festering wound;
And he cleansed off the blood with the tenderest
care;
Then he made a soft couch of the leaves on the ground,
And hastened away till assistance he found,
The suffering soldiers each homeward to bear,
Where the mother love yearned and the mother heart
bled,
And they called back to earth the spirits near fled.

A child of the Father had wandered away,
Not to loyally battle for God and the right,
But in arms as a rebel, by night and by day,
He wandered from home mid the thoughtless and gay.
He strove 'gainst the spirit with all of his might;
But the Father's great heart from the throne high above,
Went out for his child with a father's great love.

He left the bright mansions of glory on high,
And hastened to seek for the wandering child,
Who was wounded by sin and ready to die,
Not dreaming that help from One mighty was nigh.
Far, far from his home in the wilderness wild,

He lay firmly bound by the chains of the spell
Which about him were thrown by the demons of hell.

There were wounds on his feet, there were wounds on
    his head ;
  His body was bruised, until, putrid and sore,
From his head to his feet it burned angry and red,
While in anguish and pain he wished himself dead ;
  But One mighty to save sought the wilderness o'er,
While His still but sweet voice searched its depths
    through and through,
"O, sinner, your kind Father is seeking for you."

He lifts from the pit the poor, sick, wayward son,
  Takes him back to his love and a place in his heart,
While his bruises are healed by the touch of the One
Who died on the cross and salvation had won.
  In place of the old a new life they impart,
And he sings a new anthem of joy and of praise
To the Father who rescued from sin's deadly ways.

GRANDPA TAKES SELMA ONCE MORE.

You ask your old grandpa the story to tell
How we charged upon Selma, and what there befell,
Where the boom of the cannon crashed over the lea,
As the bolts of the storm-cloud flash over the sea.

We had marched many miles, but with hearts light
    and gay,
Though the foemen contested each foot of the way;

And when we looked out on the beautiful town,
We swore that her crimson-barred flag should come
    down.

But I tell you, young sir, it was no dress parade,
When they greeted our line with their hot cannonade;
There were thirty great guns in the trenches before us,
And they opened the concert in horrible chorus.

"You wish you'd been there?" you young jackanape!
Well, your granddad was there, 'cause he couldn't es-
    cape;
For I tell you, my boy, 'tis a terrible sight,
To see a division go into a fight.

But when down our line ran the oft-heard command,
"Make ready each one for a fight hand-to-hand;
Dismount from your horses and load every gun;"
We sprang to our posts and the work was begun.

Down the hill on our front, then across a ravine,
We sped double quick, making crimson the green;
For the cannon in front rained their shot and their shell
On our heads like the hail, and they aimed them right
    well.

Not a man of us halted to see what one fell,
For each one's eye was fixed on that fire-girt hell,
And we answered with cheers the artillery roar,
Though the canister shot through our bleeding ranks
    tore.

While we rallied and cheered, our hot carbines were
 ringing,
And the swift whistling balls 'mong the gunners were
 singing;
Then, with a hurrah that re-echoed afar,
We were leaping the ditches our passage to bar.

We were leaping the ditches a grave to win;
We were leaping across or falling in,
That others might make of our bodies a bridge,
To meet the brave foe on the parapet's ridge.

Now inch by the inch we were making our way,
And inch by the inch falling back the gray;
But they bartered each one for a measure of blood,
'Till the ditch was dyed red with the precious flood.

The smoke of the battle grew dense round us now,
So dense, and so heavy, my son, that I vow
Not one could quite tell, ten or twelve feet before,
As he looked at a man, what color he wore.

The sharp clashing bayonets met with a ring,
The glittering sabres did whistle and sing,
As we pushed back the foe with a purpose so set,
And planted our flag on the fort's parapet.

Soon a jolly hurrah from a great bastian floats;
It was echoed again by two thousand hoarse throats,
As they swarmed the embrasures and then leaped
 within,
Each soul all ablaze and determined to win.

As we pushed back the foe with a purpose so set,
And planted our flag on the fort's parapet.

Once over the parapet, then the sharp steel,
Drinking deeply the life-blood of rebel and leal,
Soon finished the battle so hotly begun
And established a victory gallantly won.

'Twas a glorious charge that we made, my dear boy,
And the Father of Justice there gave us the joy
Of raising Old Glory in honor once more,
On broad Alabama's most beautiful shore.

'Twas a glorious fight, but I pray God that you
May never another such battlefield know ;
And may the old flag everywhere be unfurled,
As the symbol of freedom throughout the whole world.

BLOW, BUGLER, BLOW!

Blow, bugler, blow! as you once used to blow it—
Then there was nothing to do for a poet,
Nothing, we said, but to mount and to go it
   After the graycoats, or they after us.
Sometimes 'twas one and then sometimes the other ;
Sometimes we both of us got in such pother
Which chased the other, 'twould surely much bother
   Either to tell as he mixed in the muss.

Blow the Assembly, the boys are are all ready,
None over anxious and none of them heady,
Just as they fought years ago and as steady,
  They will help settle the trouble with Spain.
They'll take the Spaniard across their lame knee, sir,
If he don't hasten with us to agree, sir,
Cuba at once shall be perfectly free, sir,
And that the dons shall quit cutting up Cain.

THE FATAL LOT.

JAMES MILLER, THE REBEL CONSCRIPT.

[War is full of sad scenes. This poem is based on the following entry in the diary of R. A. Maloney, late of Co. K, 32d Ill. veteran volunteer infantry, at the time detailed as chief clerk in Provost Marshal's office, 17th Army Corps. Mr. Maloney now, 1898, lives at Madison, Neb:

"HEADQUARTERS 17TH ARMY CORPS, DEP'T. OF TENN.
IN THE FIELD, SOUTH CAROLINA, MARCH 2, 1864.

Today Private James M. Miller, of Brown's S. C. battalion of infantry, under a lot ordered by Gen. O. O. Howard, was chosen from among the prisoners we have on hand to be shot to death in retalliation for the murder of Private Woodruff, 30th Ill. vol. infantry. The rebels had pinned a card on Woodruff's breast marked, 'Death to all Foragers.'

The prisoner was an old man and felt badly over his fate. He would not consent to my leaving him, and I staid with him to the last. After becoming composed he said that perhaps it was Divine Providence that he was selected, as he had tried to live a consistent Christian for forty years and was not afraid to die. He also said that he had not entered the rebel service until conscripted, and that he told his wife that they might force him into their service, but he would never put a bullet into his gun to fire against a United States soldier or its flag."

Mr. Maloney in writing the author calls Miller's death a murder, which it certainly was.]

'Twas down in old South Carolina many years ago
When Sherman, marching to the sea, had struck the
    fatal blow
Which staggered Johnson, shook strong Richmond's
    mighty fortress wall,
And hastened on the long wished day that brought Se-
    cession's fall.

A murdered soldier's body lay within the Union camp,
His pierced heart cold and still, his uniform with crim-
    son damp,
Not shot with arms in hand by honest, active, wily foe,
But after his surrender struck unarmed a dastard blow.

 Retaliation only such a savage foe could cause
To treat a helpless prisoner in accord with war's strict
    laws,
Which guarantee to enemies who once their weapons
    ground
Protection sure and full against all dangers lurking
    round.

For this a lot was ordered, he who drew the fatal one
Among the prisoners to be led forth at set of sun,
Dressed in his rebel uniform, though innocent, to die,
A warning menace to the fiendish murderers prowling
    nigh.

An aged man it was who met the all-appalling doom.
Appalling, for his life was sweet to him as though the
    bloom

Of youth were on his furrowed cheek ; he loved and
　　longed to live,
For life to him had many promised blessings yet to
　　give.

No coward he, yet nature shrank from such a death to
　　die.
"To-night," he said, "beneath the sod my bleeding
　　heart shall lie.
'Tis hard for shameful deeds of others I must yield my
　　life,
Like worthless dog to be shot down and not in honest
　　strife.

"I blame not your commander, for it was a murder
　　foul
Those men in rebel gray committed when, with demon
　　howl,
They so forgot a soldier's duty to a captured foe
That they could strike a wounded man unarmed a
　　deadly blow.

"But no true soldier, sir, who ever wore confederate
　　gray
Would stain a worthy soldier's shield an enemy to
　　slay.
The men were outlaws base, I know, bushwhackers
　　every one ;
The ones who fight are men ; by them such act was
　　never done.

"And now for crimes of fiends like these my blood
    must flow. Ah well,
Oft thus in war unworthy deeds of others sound the
    knell
Of him whose soul would scorn to stain an honest sol-
    dier's fame
By such an act as that which would disgrace a bandit's
    name.

"You tell me I must die, the time is very short, you say,
On me the lot has fallen and I have but time to pray.
Well, God's my faithful friend; for years I've served
    Him day and night,
And He will make the darkest hour to blaze with
    Heaven's light.

" 'Tis hard to die thus, but 'tis best perhaps that I in-
    stead
Of one all unprepared to go were called his blood to
    shed.
But comrade—let me call you such, I pray, before I
    die—
I long to see the stars and stripes o'er my loved south-
    land fly.

"You call me rebel; no 'twas cruel force that made me
    one ;
I never raised a willing hand to tear 'Old Glory' down.
Today my wife and I the stars and stripes keep hid
    away
Where we can bring it forth when comes the glorious
    better day.

"How weary we became, how sick at heart with hope deferred.
I shunned the strife as best I could till came the hated word
That I at last had drafted been for service in the field,
To fight against the flag I loved, and I was forced to yield.

"But mine is just as loyal wife as soldier ever knew,—
None braver, comrade, north or south, none to the flag more true,—
So, when the captain gave me time to say my last good bye,
We calmly talked it over while the tears bedimmed each eye.

" 'Dear James,' she said, fast holding both my hands in hers the while,
'You never trailed the dear old flag through all this wicked broil,
If forced to carry arms, my dear, 'long side of treason rank,
Ne'er place a bullet in your gun, let every shot be blank.'

"And God I call to witness, in whose presence soon I'll stand,
No union soldier ever fell in battle by my hand;
And when you captured our command upon that red hot day,
I would not try to save myself when others ran away.

"Would God that I could die for that old flag a patriot's death ;
Would I could loudly shout its praises with my latest breath ;
But, comrade, place it near to me where I can see it wave,
As 'neath your deadly volley I sink down into my grave.

"Perhaps on that last joyful day, when those who wore the blue
Salute our common Grand Commander in the great review,
The One who reads the hearts of all and knows who loyal are
Will let me march beside the blue and in your triumph share."

Perhaps 'twas right that he should die, though fate so cruel seemed ;
In view of what the foe had done his death was justice deemed ;
But, in that sunset volley's smoke, a soul went home to God
Of man as loyal to the flag as ever shed his blood.

THE BROTHERS.

"I wonder how Edward stood up 'fore the blast
That swept through our ranks and thinned them so fast,
As we dashed 'gainst the works over there, now so still,
Where the flag that we love crowns the crest of the hill.
'Twas a cruel mischance we today were denied
Our time-honored custom to fight side by side ;
And I know not if he may be lying tonight
With his face to the stars and his eyes void of light.

"My brother ! oh God ! has he fallen at last ?"
The speaker had stopped, and was gazing aghast
At a heap on the ground of the dying and dead ;
Then quickly he stooped, and raising the head
Of one who lay bleeding and moaning with pain,
Struck low where the missiles had fallen like rain,
He peered in his bloodless and powder-streaked face,
Once with life all aglow and with strong manly grace.

"Why, Fred, this is you ; take a generous pull
At this well-filled canteen, draw away till you're full.
Let me see where it struck. Was it minnie or shell
Tore this hole in your leg ? Let me bandage it. Well,
And now where is Ed ? Was he still on his feet
When the grape flew so hot our stern column to greet,
And piled dying and dead in this crimson-dyed heap,
As if treason were precious while life were most cheap ?

"He was standing, you tell me, now thanks be to God!"
Then he sprang to his feet and still onward he plod,
Peering into dead faces, yet filled with the dread
Lest a brother's loved form lay there silent and dead.
"Ah, that is his cap—no, 'tis poor Charlie Snell,
Struck down at his post with a fragment of shell.
See how thickly they lie all about—can it be
That my brother escaped where such havoc I see?

"How well I remember that day when I found
That Ed had enlisted, been accepted as sound,
And that soon, in defense of the red white and blue,
He would march to the front where the rifle-balls flew.
To prevent him from going, I tried every art,
And when other means failed I appealed to his heart,
Told of mother's heart crushed, but, alas, 'twas in vain,
Though his face was convulsed with a spasm of pain.

"Then I tried—how I blush such a crime to confess—
Yes, I meant to deceive him, yet none would dare guess
That the son of my father and a mother as true
To the flag as e'er breathed 'neath the heavenly blue,
Before all the world would the falsehood proclaim
That he hated the flag, and ne'er crimson with shame.
Well, I did blush, but anger oft leads us to say
What we wish were unsaid e'er the close of the day.

"I said that a copperhead I was henceforth;
But I lied when I said it that day in the north;
My soul felt the stigma, my cheek burned with shame,
As my own lips applied to myself the foul name.

I was mad when I uttered the terrible word,
And I'm glad that no other the falsehood e'er heard
Than the brother who loved me and knew none more true
Could be found than was I to the red white and blue."

"Ah, Will," he gave answer, "your heart never spoke
Those words you have uttered ; 'twas only a joke,
For I know that no traitor e'er sprang from the stock,
Whose ancestry brought freedom's foes to the block.
But, Will, were it true that the old homestead tree
Gave shade to a foe to the flag of the free,
Then a thousand fold more upon me rests the claim
To rescue your patriot father's fair name."

"So he donned his new uniform, gave a last kiss
To the mother who bore him and gloried in this,
That she had a son of her own she could give
That treason might die and the nation might live.
I followed, of course ; for with zeal my soul burned
To wipe out the stain, as I thought how I spurned
The cry of distress, as my country did plead
With her children to help in her desperate need.

"But who is that moving with soft careful tread
O'er this torn, bloody field among dying and dead?
Why, yes, that is Ed and he's looking for me,
And he thinks he has found me there under that tree.
Ho, Ed, what's the matter? Is anything lost?"
"Hello ! Will, my boy, I was counting the cost."
Both knew, as they stood clasping hands 'neath the tree,
That a true brother's love is a fathomless sea.

CHARGE OF MINTY'S BRIGADE.

Lovejoy Station, Ga , Aug. 19, 1864

Trapped was the wary, but fearless Kilpatrick,
   Sorely beset by a jubilant foe,
Pouring their broadsides from front, flank and rearward,
   Eager to crush the old fox at a blow.
        Hear that exultant cheer,
        As they on flank appear.
Reynolds has massed a division in front of him ;
   Cleburn comes down at the right on the run ;
Jackson, on left and in rear with his batteries,
   Hurls shot and shell from full many a gun.

"Must they surrender ?" some timid ones query ;
   "Never," cries Minty, "while I have a blade ;
"Give but the word and we carve out a pathway,
   "I and my men of the old first brigade."
        "Forward the first brigade ;
        "Charge yonder barricade."
This the reply of the swift acting leader,
   While like an arrow shot out from the bow,
Minty's brigade leaps forth on their mission,
   Each trooper's bosom with ardor aglow.

Over the hill dash the galloping squadrons,
   Striking a chill to the hearts of the foe ;
Glittering sabers now throw back the sunlight,
   Then in warm lifeblood they dim their bright glow.

Wide spreading gaps are made,
By the fierce cannonade,
Shaking the earth and obscuring the heavens.
Still rides that line of steel, flashing its wrath ;
Like mountain avalanche onward it thunders,
Hurling to death all that stands in its path.

Ten thousand men rolling volleys are pouring
Into the ranks that in unequal fight,
Dared yet to charge on the enemy boldly,
Though there were six to their one now in sight.
Facing such metal rain,
Valor seems all in vain.
Murderous shell are exploding about them,
Whistling minnie balls scream through the air,
Emptying saddles and staining the greensward,
Oh the brave hearts that are perishing there !

Yet the bold horsemen are eagerly pressing
In where the barricade Jackson doth shield ;
Sabers are whirling in circles above them,
Armed with the vengeance which patriots wield.
Crash, and the lines are met ;
Sabers with blood are wet ;
Steel has met steel and is drinking the lifeblood ;
Horses and riders in heaps strew the ground ;
Rifle and pistol shot whistling about them,
Tear through the air, volleyed round upon round.

List to the ringing steel clash the opposing steel,
Twining like serpents in deadly embrace,
Parrying, thrusting, and striking to right and left,

Sabers are whirling in circles above them,
Armed with the vengeance which patriots wield.

Hewing men down without pity or grace.
    Oh, what a day of woe
    This to the sullen foe !
Scores of their bravest struck down 'neath the saber
    stroke,
  Cover the ground on every side ;
Cannon, o'erturned, or with carriage and caisson broke,
  Belch no more fire of death far and wide.

Minty is hewing his way at the forefront ;
  Swift McIntyre has taken a gun ;
Baily's own hand too has taken another ;
  Every bold trooper has prodigies done.
    Stop the tornado ;
    Block up its way, though
Cherish no thought this swift torrent of stemming;
  Minty's brigade will not be denied.
What though an army should block up the pathway ;
  It shall be swept far away by the tide.

Still goes the clamor on ; still flows the crimson tide ;
  Still sways the deadly strife hither and yon.
"Strike, for Old Glory, boys ; down with the stars
    and bars ;
  "You have a road to win—it must be won."
    Hark, yonder loud hurrah !
    Victory's proud huzza !
See the once stubborn foe broken asunder,
  Shattered and bleeding, now flee far away.
Sheath your red sabers ; your duty is ended,
  Safe lies the path, you have won the proud day.

WILL AND NELLIE.

Ma, they tell me that Willie is coming,
The one whom they call Willie Brace;
Yes, he wrote me the news in a letter,
And a blush mantled sweet Nellie's face;
For one day
       In the May,
              'Neath the tree
                      On the lea,
Will had whispered the story as old as the race;
The story of love she had happily heard,
For it found a response though she said not a word.

On that day she was only a lassie,
A pledge of the woman to be;
For 'twas only her seventeenth birthday,
And an eighteen years' boy was he.
But he stood
       Like a good
            loyal knight
                      In her sight,
In his blue regimentals; then, bending his knee,
He had poured out his love for the beautiful maid,
And his strong manly heart at her feet he had laid.

"Dearest Nell, they may say we are children
And know not the wish of our heart;
But I know that my heart is now bleeding,

As from your dear side I depart.
If I stand
      Like a man,
             To the blue
                    Ever true,
Can I ask you to pledge me today e'er I start
That, when homeward I come from the red field of strife,
You will come to my side as my bonnie sweet wife?"

And Nellie had answered him sweetly,
As, placing her hand in his own,
She looked in his manly face proudly,
While lovelight from out her heart shone:
"Who will fight
      For the right
           And this grand
                Native land,
Is no longer a child, but a man fully grown;
And he pleads not in vain with the maid of his choice,
For his deeds plead his cause with an eloquent voice."

Oh the sad, weary days she had waited,
Her heart with suspense ever torn;
Today it would leap strong and hopeful,
Then sink in its anguish forlorn.
As she read
      Of the dead,
           She had dreamed,
                Till it seemed
That her far away lover of life had been shorn;
Yet through all those dark days was her heart ever true,
And she longed the return of her lover in blue.

He had marched through the swamps and the forest ;
He had climbed o'er the steep mountain wall ;
He had stood in the forefront of battle,
And had seen many brave comrades fall.
As a rock
        Meets the shock
                And hurls back
                        On its track
The great wave in its wrath towering high over all,
So had Willie's brave regiment stood by the flag,
As they planted it high on the mountain's top crag.

She had heard how he lifted the banner,
When the bearer a shell had laid low,
How he sprang to the front where the grapeshot
Felled a hundred or more at one blow,
How he stood
        Where the blood
                Of the slain
                        Did enstain
Every foot of the soil with its copious flow ;
Then rang out his fierce shout as o'er ramparts he sprang,
And the victor's huzza through the murky air rang.

And today he was home again marching—
List, 'tis surely the drum that she hears ;
Now her heart is exultingly bounding,
Then sinks with a maiden's coy fears.
Will he too
        Still be true
                Even now
                        To the vow

That he made to her then, e'er these long, weary years?
Then she chided her heart that so much as in thought
It had doubted when he had so loyally fought.

But the music drew rapidly nearer;
She heard the quick tramping of feet,
Then she saw the bronzed veterans passing,
They marched down the city's broad street;
Till at last
        He marched past,
                Bronzed and browned
                        By the sun,
The one hero her heart was impatient to meet;
And she blushed like a rose as he passed where she sat
And smiled on her proudly and lifted his hat.

"Break ranks!" and they hastened to scatter,
Each eager to seek the old home
And to kiss once again the dear loved ones,
No more from the fireside to roam.
With a thrill,
        Gallant Will,
                Full of pride,
                        Reached the side
Of sweet Nell, who from under the rooftree had come,
To greet and to welcome the one that she loved,
Who in forefront of battle his manhood had proved.

"May I claim, my dear love, the fulfillment
Of pledges you made that dark day,
When I marched to the front as a soldier,
To serve in the midst of the fray?"

Then a smile
      Void of guile
           Added grace
                  To her face,
As arm within arm they hastened away.
"Who has loyally fought for the red white and blue,
Need never to doubt that my love will be true."

Many years have sped by since the soldier
Returned from the camp and the field ;
His musket hangs rusty and useless ;
The muster roll long has been sealed.
But beside
      His fond bride,
           Prouder none
                'Neath the sun.
The years have the worth of the lovers revealed.
Bonnie Nell is a matron ; her boys are all true
To the Flag of the Union, the Red White and Blue.

A SENTIMENT.

Could I cull from all bards every beautiful thought,
Every strong burning sentence with loyalty fraught ;
Could some potent alembic their essence condense
Into one rich expression of fragrance intense ;
I would dedicate this to the flag that I love,
The flag that I pray may float ever above
Every mountain and plain this whole continent o'er,
And the beautiful islands that fringe her fair shore.

A TRIBUTE TO MY WIFE.

I courted her once for her beauty,
    Not alone of form and face,
Though, to eye of her true hearted lover,
    Of each there was more than a trace.
I was sure that the rogue truly loved me,
    But for years she would never confess;
So I courted and courted and courted,
    While her secret I tried hard to guess.

But I knew 'twould come out in due season,
    And so, in due season, it did,
And I found, as I'd dreamed, that she loved me,
    E'en when 'twas so cunningly hid.
But I quickly forgave the young torment
    The fiction she acted so well,
It had only drawn closer the meshes
    That wove about me a sweet spell.

Since then I have courted her daily
    For more than a score of bright years,
And I know that she still loves me truly—
    No room for more doubtings or fears.
And if the kind father will spare us
    Another full score or two more,
I'll begin the whole love story over.
    And do all my past courting o'er.

And when the bright angel hosts call us,
　　Whichever is first one to go,
Will watch by the pearly white portal
　　Till the other comes up from below;
And then I will gather the flowers
　　That grow by the river of life,
Through eternity's unnumbered ages,
　　Arm in arm with my darling sweet wife.

For true love is surely immortal,
　　And ours has always been true.
The body may sleep in the valley,
　　The soul will mount up through the blue;
And love shall live on through the ages,
　　Where nothing its beauties can mar,
Of all the bright heavenly glories,
　　The richest and far brightest star.

THE BUGLER.

How he made the echoes jingle!
How our ears did roar and tingle!
How we swore, I dare not tell ye,
As we heard the loud reveille,
All our lovely dreams ignoring,
Bidding each to quit his snoring,
Roll his blanket, don his breeches,
Quick enough to rip the stitches.

Some fool picket's touched the trigger—
Got a bite from boring jigger—
Toot the bugle goes like blazes
Till the dead it almost raises;
Out we go to saddle springing,
Carbines loaded, sabers ringing,
Ride a mile, perhaps a dozen,
Then come back the picket cussin'.

Sometimes bugler blew for rations,
Quickly then we took our stations,
Half or full when we could get them—
Commissaries never fret them—
Haversacks then quickly grabbing,
Coffee bags into them jabbing,
Double quick and sometimes quicker,
Each one had some grub to dicker.

Well we knew when came our letters,
That old bugle had the stutters;
Notes came fast and faster racing,
Each the former headlong chasing;
Bugler's heart all in a flurry.
We all knew what made him hurry,
His true sweetheart near forgot him,
Every mail a letter brought him.

Mid the battle field's loud clanging,
Where the smoke was heavy hanging,
Death shots falling, thickly falling—
Mid the clamor so appalling,

By his colonel, firm and steady,
Stood that bugler, ever ready ;
High the swelling notes e'er floated,
From that trumpet, brazen-throated.

That old bugler with his braying
Made us feel not much like praying ;
Blew to get up, blew to pack up—
Sometimes we just got our back up—
Blew for breakfast, blew to saddle,
How he made us fellows paddle,
And I'll bet if he's now going,
That blamed bugler still is blowing.

When the trumpet call is pealing,
End of time to all revealing,
I'm not sure, but I'm surmising
That our bugler, quickly rising,
From his grave alertly bounding,
As he hears reveille sounding,
Will a peal send o'er the valley
That the veterans will rally.

DRESS BY THE FLAG.

A cyclone of death was fast sweeping the field,
    Where a column for victory was toiling ;
And it seemed that before it the column must yield,
    For the men were already recoiling,

In a hundred hard battles each soldier had stood
    Like a rock, the fierce storm cloud defying,
And crimsoned the green with the foeman's best blood,
    Or had sent him for safety a-flying.

But the terrible guns swept each foot of the hill,
    With precision and havoc appalling,
Hurling canister shot and great grapeshot as well,
    And the heroes were rapidly falling;
For not one could live on that cleanly mown trail,
    Which the besom of death was now sweeping;
And back they recoiled out of reach of the gale,
    That its horrible harvest was reaping.

Then a soldier sprang out from the storm-riven line,
    His challenge defiantly flinging,
The banner he grasped, and rushed up the incline,
    A wild cheer setting echoes a-ringing:
"Dress up to the flag; move forward, my boys;
    Align once again by 'Old Glory';
We will sweep yonder hills of its dangerous toys,
    Or we'll leave this red slope the more gory."

With a shout like the sound of Niagara's roar,
    As over the cliff she falls dashing,
They rallied again and aligned them once more,
    Where the shot and the shell were still crashing;
Then on toward the hilltop exulting they pressed,
    And soon the great guns they were spiking,
As, leaping the trenches. they swept o'er the crest,
    Dismay to each foeman's heart striking.

How oft, when the victory nearly is won,
    We recoil from the strife yet before us,
And the cause that we love is near lost and undone,
    While the foe sings in jubilant chorus.
How we long for a leader, both loyal and true,
    With a hero's complete consecration,
To shout, as he lifts our loved ensign to view,
    "Come each by the flag take your station."

When our hopes for the future in jeopardy lie,
    And the foeman's great armies engirt us ;
When reforms we have cherished seem born but to die,
    And our followers haste to desert us ;
Let a man who dare fall in defense of the right
    Sieze hold of the flagstaff so slender,
And cry dashing into the thick of the fight,
    "By the banner, right dress, each defender."

But who shall that hero be, lifting the flag
    Far ahead of the laggards who tarry?
Say, whence shall he come, fellow-man, if thou lag,
    Who ought that same banner to carry?
Why others win laurels your own brow should wear?
    Duty calls, and it calls on you loudly,
Sieze the flag e'er it fall, and then fearlessly bear
    It in front of the column most proudly.

But see, they have planted the flag of reform
    On mountain, on hilltop, in valley,
Where the bearers alone are now breasting the storm,
    And are calling the nations to rally.

Haste you, dress by the flag and stand up like a man
  And your part in the conflict be taking,
Though another is bearer, be found in the van,
  Where the bugle the echoes are waking.

Dress straight by the banner in every reform ;
  Every peril in front be thou sharing ;
Never lag with the ambulance, safe from all harm ;
  Be in line with the heroes most daring.
Only thus canst thou merit the master's "well done,"
  When he comes the true heroes rewarding ;
But though humble your part, he will never pass one,
  Who stood where the flag needed guarding.

THE VETERAN AND THE FLAG.

"Stranger, can you show a soldier
  The old banner that he bore
Mid the furious strife of battle,
  Where the cannon loud did roar?
Somewhere in this massive building
  They have stored the battle flags,
Torn and stained, with colors faded,
  Some in ribbons, some in rags.

"But, though still remains but little
  Of the glory of the stars,
Let me once more see the ensign
  That outwaved the stars and bars.

I was once the banner bearer
  Of the regiment you see,
And 'twas there I lost this leg, sir,
  Torn away just at the knee.

"Ah, that day grew hot and hotter,
  And the crimson tide ran deep,
As the Johnnies charged our columns,
  Toiling up the hillside steep.
'Twas before that queenly city,
  Nestled mid the Georgia hills,
Proud Atlanta—how that name, sir,
  Still my inmost bosom thrills!

"On that day the foe seemed desperate,
  Bound to break our line of steel,
And they dashed their weight against us,
  Till they made our columns reel;
But we rained the lead upon them
  In a sharp and deadly sleet,
Cutting down their whole divisions,
  As the reaper lays the wheat.

"Soon I felt a shock that dazed me,
  And the flag fell at my feet,
While this arm hung limp and bleeding,
  And my heart near ceased to beat.
But I grasped the proud old banner
  E'er 'twere touched by other hands,
And I waved it in defiance
  In the face of Hood's command.

"Then—I know not how it was, sir—
　　I had fallen in a heap,
That old flag beneath my body,
　　As the grape our line did sweep.
When I tried, my feet regaining,
　　Once again the flag to hold,
This good leg was gone forever,
　　And my blood had stained each fold.

"From the field my comrades bore me,
　　While I cheered, as best I could,
The old flag that others lifted,
　　And shook out in face of Hood.
As a mother loves her first-born,
　　As a father loves his heir,
Comrade, I revere that banner,
　　For my blood has stained it there."

"Come, my comrade," said the stranger,
　　Going on the man before ;
Then, into a spacious hallway,
　　Open wide he threw the door.
There, revealed in all their grandeur,
　　Were the trophies of the field,
Where the boys who wore the azure
　　Forced the traitor gray to yield.

But the chiefest sight to patriot
　　Were the flags, all stained and rent,
Which, amid the smoke of conflict,
　　Crowned each trench and battlement.

In a case, kept locked securely,
    Flags by scores and hundreds stood ;
Some were torn and hung in fragments,
    Some were stained with human blood.

"Where's the banner of the Second ?—
    Sight, you see, is failing me—
Yet I think that I would know it,
    Though a thousand I should see.
Ah ! behold ! there stands Old Glory ;
    Let us give her three times three."
Then, on high his brown hat swinging,
    Cheer on cheer pealed loyally.

"Now, my comrade, for I see, sir,
    That the button decks your vest,
Let me grasp once more the ensign
    That's enshrined within my breast ;
Let me kiss the faded Union ;
    Let me press it to my heart ;
Let me wave it once above me,
    E'er forever we must part.

"What ! 'I cannot,' do you tell me?
    'It is 'gainst the express command?
It is old and will not bear it
    To be touched by careless hand?'
Comrade, see this sleeve, now empty,
    See this cane my steps to aid ;
Think you not I know the value
    Of the flag, and how 'twas paid?

"Comrade, these I gave to save it
   From dishonor and disgrace,
Bathed it with my own rich life blood—
   See it there in that dark place,
I will touch the time stained colors
   With a tenderest lover's care ;
Not a thread shall e'er be broken,
   If you heed my earnest prayer."

From its place among the trophies
   Of a thousand fields hard won,
Came the torn and blackened banner,
   Once again to greet the sun.
Flashed his eye with fire olden,
   Flushed his cheek with manly pride ;
Then he placed his arm about it
   Gently, as it were his bride.

"Dear old flag, once more I see you,"
   Came in broken sobs his voice,
"Crowned with victory and honor.
   How it makes my heart rejoice !"
Slowly he unwound the banner
   From its staff of ashen wood,
Till, revealed, a spot of blackness
   Showed the stain of human blood.

"Hail ! Old flag, again I greet you,
   Last in battle smoke beheld,
Where the thunderous cannon's booming
   Treason's doom forever knelled.

You and I are growing older,
  Soon this battered hulk shall lie
'Neath the lilies of the valley,
  While my soul shall upward fly.

"But, old flag, although this body
  Gave a leg, and one good arm,
It has yet of each another,
  Pledged to shield you from all harm.
May the blight of heaven's curses
  Fall upon the soul of him
Who e'er dares to raise a finger,
  Star or stripe to erase or dim."

FIGHT IT OUT ON THIS LINE.

In the battle of life there are struggles
  That test every power of soul,
And too often the ones we confide in
  Would turn us aside from the goal;
But, when false advisers would swerve us
  From pushing right up each incline,
Be this our firm, confident answer:
  "I shall fight to the end on this line."

If difficulties thicken about you
  And challenge your right to proceed,
If mountains block up the straight pathway,
  While side-tracks around them would lead,

Don't swerve from your purpose a hair's breadth;
   I charge you 'tis better, in fine,
Though tunnels must pierce the hard granite,
   To blast the rocks through on this line.

The side tracks lead down through the valley,
   And lower and lower will run,
While you must climb higher and higher,
   To win the approving, "Well done";
And so, though the crags hang above you,
   And steep is the mountain's incline,
You will do the best thing, I assure you,
   To climb toward the stars on this line.

There is many a road that seems easier,
   When you are not going that way,
And battles you daily are fighting
   Will seem to you never to pay;
But distance it is lends enchantment,
   And, my son, it will not do to whine;
For, if ever you really get there,
   You will have to stick close to this line.

You are now in the front of the battle,
   All armed from your head to your feet,
A good knight with the vows of the Templar,
   Going forth a bold foeman to meet;
There are hundreds of ways to attack him,
   By flanking, by charge, or by mine;
But let others choose each his own method;
   You will find enough work on this line.

You may not strike hard blows at the center;
　His flank you may still fail to turn;
No fortress may haul down its colors;
　The citadel you may not burn;
But, if you just tear up the railroad
　That furnishes crackers and wine,
And cut off all fresh reenforcements,
　You'll have done a good work on this line.

There are rivers to cross on your marches,
　Without either bridge or pontoon;
And you must oft cross them by wading,
　Or sometimes by playing the loon,
And swimming or diving, as may be;
　But still, my dear boy, I opine
That water is good to refresh you;
　'Twill not pay you to seek a new line.

The generals who have won honors,
　The statesmen who blessed all their kind,
Reformers of all climes and ages,
　Were never the sport of the wind;
Though impossibilities faced them,
　They each of dismay gave no sign,
But whistled a tune and pushed onward,
　And ne'er made a crook in the line.

Rest assured that no work is accomplished
　By constantly changing your base;
For, while you are shifting supply trains,
　The foe will outrun in the race.

So in the great contests before you,
    E'en though you must swim the broad Rhine,
If you have half the soul of a hero,
    Strike out for yon shore a bee line.

ONE BY ONE.

One by one the old comrades are falling,
    Falling like leaves that have dropped by the way,
As each has heard the Great Captain's voice calling,
    Summoning home to the regions of day.
Once, at our side in the smoke of the battle,
Stood they amidst the sharp musketry rattle,
    Keeping the foes of their country at bay.

Then their proud step was elastic and springing,
    Full of the vigor of youth, quick and strong ;
Each manly voice was both robust and ringing,
    Raised in defense of the right 'gainst the wrong ;
Bravely they charged where the minnie balls sang ;
Loud as their rifles their challenges rang ;
    While 'neath the flag they were marching along.

Comrades in arms in a conflict most holy,
    Battling a nation's existence to save,
Though many sprang from a parentage lowly,
    Millions of hearts bend in love o'er each grave.
In the great struggle each one did his best,
Bore well his burden, than sank to his rest,
    Loved by the fairest, and wept by the brave.

Wearily home from the field of their glory,
    Marched they abreast in those sad days of yore ;
Some had left limbs on the battlefield gory ;
    Some racked with pain, reached the old homestead door;
Some were borne down by the weight of disease,
Found in the swamps or far out on the seas,
    Heirlooms of burdens and labors they bore.

Broken are ranks that were once firm and serried,
    When beat the hailstones of death in their face,
While to the onset each patriot hurried,
    Keeping step firmly and marching in place.
Time is fast turning above them the sod—
On many coffins has fallen the clod,
    Sod, clod, nor coffin our love can efface.

Gather, old comrades, about each green mound,
    Where our dear brothers are lying today ;
Raise the old flag o'er the hallowed ground,
    Where they are sleeping the ages away ;
Bring from earth's treasures the loveliest flowers,
Culled from the hillsides, the valleys and bowers ;
    Cover them o'er with these jewels of May.

Swear on their tombstones each veteran's son,
    True to their memory ever to be,
Each to maintain what their fathers have won,
    Each to defend the dear flag of the free.
Sons of the veterans, yours the disgrace,
Should a bold traitor but one star erase
    From the proud ensign they leave you today.

JIM.

"Excuse me, mister, 'cause my pants is ragged jest a bit;
An' this ol' hat was once my pa's, it isn't quite a fit;
But's best I have, an' what's the use o' shiverin' with the cold,
An' throwin' 'way the best ye got, jest 'cause its pretty old?
'My coat?' well, yes, it's mine, though somewhat ragged, I confess;
But better far nor nothin' sir, against the storm, I guess.
It doesn't fit me none too well; I'll hev to grow awhile
To fill it, fer it's papa's coat, an' somewhat out of style.

" 'Who is my papa?' Well, now, say, 'tis strange that you don't know
The man who fit at Richmond more nor thirty years ago,
Who dug the mine at Petersburg that blew the rebs sky high,
Then dashed into the awful pit jest bound to whip or die.
His name was Jim—same's mine is, sir—Jim Brown, of Company B.
'His regiment?' Don't know now, but the one that whipped Bob Lee.

You know which one it was, sir, 'cause you must have been a man,
When that big fight was on down there, so tell me if you can.

" 'Twas long 'fore I was born, you know, that tussle was fought out—
I'd like to seen it, an' I would if I had been about;
But then I wa'n't; I didn't come for twenty year an' more;
For when this little chick was born the war had long been o'er.
But pa was there—say, mister, shout an' swing your tall silk tile.
Let's give the flag a rousin' cheer they'll hear for more'n a mile;
For that's the flag my papa loved, for it he fought an bled;
We wrapped its folds around him sir, when he was cold an' dead.

"Yes, he is dead; the awful wound he got that bloody day
At Petersburg, when his command dashed yellin' at the gray—
You see 'twas jest like this, sir—p'r'aps you've heard it told before.
'No?' Well that's strange at your age, for they've told it o'er an' o'er.
Well, papa, he was 'mong the first to reach the parapet,
As our boys pushed the rebels back at point of bayonet,

When, sir, a grapeshot tore a hole clean through my
    papa's side.
If he'd 'a been some men, sir, he'd laid down then an'
    died.

"But pa was grit, now, well he was, an' druv grim
    death away ;
He meant to stay awhile an' fight the rebs some other
    day.
An' sure's you re born he did git well, an' he was with
    our men
When Lee pulled down the stars an' bars to never float
    again.
But that big wound kep' breakin' out, an' papa
    couldn't work—
He did his best though, mister, 'cause my papa was no
    shirk—
An' then he got his pension, but it wasn't half enough
To feed us all an' clothe us, so we had it pretty tough.

"But papa did too much, an' day by day he paler grew,
Yet no complaint to us he made, an' no one scarcely
    knew
The way he suffered, till at last the angels took him
    home
An' left my ma an' Joe an' me to fight it out alone.
An' then the pension stopped, you see, an' mamma,
    she took sick,
An' troubles came upon our home so awful, awful
    thick.
I tried, an' so did Joey, sir, to see what we could do,
To help her earn enough to eat an' beat the winter
    through.

"But 'twas a pretty rustlin' job fer two sech boys as we,
Fer mamma she kep' sick in bed for weeks an' weeks, you see.
We couldn't buy us any clo's, so Joe took papa's shoes,
An' I his hat an' coat an' pants, his worn out army blues.
But here comes Joe; hello, what's that you say? Don't play no trick.
'You h'ain't? Ma's pension's come,' you say? Well, Uncle Sam's a brick.
I'm glad for ma, she needs it so, to pay the doctor's bill,
An' get her somethin' good to take to stop that awful chill.

An' mister, some o' these comin' days this number two Jim Brown
Will don a bran new uniform, an' where the cannon soun'
He'll spot the Spaniard or the Turk or any other one
Who dares to try to bully us or pull ol' Glory down.
He'll shoulder papa's rusty gun—It's full of danger yet
To any foe to that ol' flag that papa loved, you bet—
An' Young Jim Brown will do his best to give them fellers fits
An' knock their ships an' guns an' things to more'n a million bits.

THE GRAY'S LAST CAMPAIGN.

The Blue and the Gray, like two quarrelsome boys,
Once disputed and fought o'er some baubles and toys;
They both got their eyes blackened as black as could be,
Till their eyelids were closed and they hardly could see;
But the Blue being strongest, the Graycoat was licked,
And it stuck in his crop for his pride was sore pricked.

There were stains on the green in that time long ago,
Where the blood of the Blue and the Gray did outflow;
There were charge and retreat, and the hot countercharge;
There were thunders of cannon where Gray was the targe;
There were answering peals, when the Bluecoat went down
Where the canister shot had a passage way mown.

But the Gray once again is seen marching along,
And he comes not with yells, but sweet charity's song—
From Atlanta to sea Sherman's bummers once pressed;
From Atlanta the Grays have marched clear to the west,
With an offering of peace and a pledge of good will,
From the field and the garden, the mine and the mill.

Nebraska is taken, her capital lies
At the feet of the Johnnies, a fully earned prize;
Let us open the gates of each town on the plain,
For those Grays, if we don't, will be cutting up Cain.
No use to skedaddle, my comrades, I vow,
For the old soldier state surely's in for it now.

We surrender, brave Grays, and up goes the white flag ;
You have captured us sure, we have nothing to brag ;
When you fired your cartridges loaded with flour,
You hit us right smart, and it hurt us a power ;
And we reckon, my boys, though Atlanta we took,
You have gobbled us Yankees this time like a book.

But we'll stir up a blizzard to blockade the road,
And force them to make this good state their abode ;
We'll burn every bridge and demolish the track,
For I vum those brave Johnnies shall never go back ;
We'll let loose our cowboys to capture the train,
E'er we let those kind Graycoats go southward again.

God bless the brave Southland's great generous heart,
As she comes to the West needed aid to impart ;
They have ridden clean down the last hardness we had ;
It's impossible more to keep righteously mad.
Clasp hands, gallant Grays o'er the gulf of the past ;
May the racket we had, as our first, be our last.

THE DRUMMER BOY'S DIRGE.

Roll, roll, roll,
Over the grave of the drummer boy dead ;
Beat the drum softly there by his bed ;
Roll, roll it tenderly over his head ;
Roll, roll, roll.

Roll, roll, roll,
Once and again as the ages go by ;
Roll till the reveille call from on high
Sounds to awake him to mount to the sky ;
Roll, roll, roll.

Hang high his drum in the temple of fame ;
Write on her tablets the drummer boy's name,
Garlanded round with the oak leaf and bay,
While he is sleeping the ages away.

ALL QUIET ON THE POTOMAC.

No more the sound of fife and drum ;
    No more the cannon's crashing ;
No more the rifle bullet's hum ;
    No more the saber's clashing,
The fires of hate no longer burn,
Nor north nor south each other spurn.

Once hostile armies tramped the banks ;
    Once hung the smoke of battle
O'er angry men in serried ranks,
    Beneath, the musket's rattle.
Alas ! alas ! 'Twas brothers stood
Each thristing for the other's blood.

A better day has come at last ;
    A brighter sun has risen.
The day of hate forever past,
    Today fulfills the vision

Our nation's seers, with souls aglow,
Saw down the vista long ago.

The fratricidal war is o'er ;
    The reeking swords are broken ;
The clash of arms is heard no more,
    Of bloody strife the token.
"All quiet," said we ? no, the whirr
Of wheels replace the crash of war.

The peaceful spindles softly sing
    Their quiet little ditty,
The chiming church bells—hear them ring,
    In hamlet and in city.
A happy people live today
Where once the Blue defied the Gray.

In halls of congress now behold,
    In friendly emulation,
The men whose deadly volleys rolled
    In angry altercation
Today with earnest, loyal zeal
They seek their common country's weal.

Ah, happy nation thus to see
    The bonds of love cemented.
A mighty people yet to be
    Shall dwell here, and contented.
On this foundation they shall build
Till promised greatness is fulfilled.

BE NOT DISMAYED.

Be not dismayed, if 'tis thy lot
To suffer scorn where thou ought not;
   The world is slow the worth to see
   Of him who scorns to bend his knee
To despot king, to wealth, or ought
But God; who stands a man unbought,
   And faces fierce detraction's storm,
   A foe to sin in any form.
One age the Maid of Orleans burns;
And France her cry for mercy spurns,
   For whom she struck such stalwart blow,
   The France she freed from foreign foe.
Another age bids sculptor's art
To adorn the city's thronging mart
   With monumental pile to tell
   How she who freed them nobly fell.
They canonize and dub a saint
The one for witchcraft then attaint.
   Because oppression he defied,
   John Brown upon the scaffold died;
But still his soul went marching on
Until the work was fully done
   Which stirred his heart, his courage fired,
   And sacrificial zeal inspired.
A traitor then, a hero now,
We place the laurel on his brow.

'Tis always thus. The mad mob howl
And crucify the noble soul
Who dares to lead, if need be die,
Where cringeing cowards duty fly.
  Act well thy part ; thy duty do ;
  Thy country serve ; to God be true.
Leave all the rest to time and Him
Who gives the crown that naught can dim.
  That crown is sure ; and man who wrongs
  Your praise may sing in future songs.

THE COMPACT OF THE BLUE AND THE GRAY.

We boys of the Blue and we boys of the Gray
A compact have made with each other today ;
Both sworn to the old stars and stripes to be true,
We shoulder to shoulder shall march hitherto ;
Though it's not always been thus as all people know,
For we had an unpleasantness some time ago.

We boys of the Gray—well, we still love "Old Glory",
Though we fully confess that on fields that were gory
We did the old flag of some stars try to rob—
We hadn't a notion we had such a job—
If we had that same contract again we would quit
Before ever a Blue or a Gray had been hit.

We then wanted a part of the flag that was borne
By Sumpter and Marion in freedom's glad morn ;

So we thought we'd pluck out near a dozen bright stars
And borrow a few of her stripes for our bars
And then stitch them together as well as we might
And call it a flag for which we could fight.

The strong union bunting our efforts defied,
But 'twas not until more than a million had died
We relinquished an effort so wondrously great
To try for the old a new flag to create
And decided to rally again 'neath the one
Under which our forefathers made Britishers run.

We boys of the blue greet as comrades today
The boys that we fought while wearing the gray.
We march under one flag, the most beautiful one
That was ever unfurled anywhere 'neath the sun ;
We were proud of the gray when in battle we met ;
Now they stand for the flag, we are far prouder yet.

We are none of us worth for a fight very much,
As we hobble along with a cane or a crutch,
But we're ready to go and to do what we can ;
To Columbia's flag we'd be true to a man,
For we know but one banner, the red white and blue,
And the Blue and the Gray to that flag are both true.

The nation that dares any insult to fling
At that old starry banner whose praises we sing,
Or which comes to these shores with its armies arrayed,
Its power to show and the land to invade,
Be its cause right or wrong, be its strength what it may,
Must walk over the bodies of the Blue and of Gray.

CHARLES CARROLL OF CARROLLTON.

A tyrant was plotting against a free land,
All freedom to crush with a merciless hand,
While as slaves he had branded a brave freeborn race ;
But they hurled their defiance back into his face,
For men were full men in those stern days of yore,
And the strong, stalwart sons of the forest all swore
That the last drop of blood from their hearts should be torn,
E'er the gyves of a tyrant by freemen were worn.

And when the time came that the vow must be paid,
None shirked, and his duty none tried to evade ;
But with rifle or musket, whate'er they possessed,
They marched to the conflict from east and from west :
Then they stood like a wall made of full tempered steel,
While their broadsides, well aimed, caused the tyrant to reel,
And, ragged and hungry, their banner unfurled,
And fired the shots that were heard round the world.

And then with hearts burning with eager desire,
Their great souls all ablaze with the patriot fire,
Each sworn to do all his dear country to save,
Congress sent the bold challenge across the broad wave,
Which declared to the tyrant in words understood,
That though they were kin, of the same Saxon blood,
He had forfeited claim their allegiance to hold,
Because he had robbed them of birthright and gold.

Then each stood in his place as the long roll was called—
Not a delegate flinched and not one stood appalled—
And declared that henceforth and forever and aye
This nation to tyrants no more should be prey ;
That the colonies are, and of right ought to be,
Independent of all, and the home of the free ;
While they pledged to each other their lives and their all,
And their honor, together to stand or to fall.

And then—write their names on the tablet of fame !—
To the great declaration they subscribed each his name ;
But, when Carroll had written, in bold, open hand,
His name to the paper which cut every band,
Another spoke out in a banter and jest,
"The Carrolls are many, and, mid all the rest,
Charles Carroll, the rebel, can never be found
When the hangman for victims is looking around."

The eye of the patriot flashed with the fire
That illumined his soul and rose higher and higher,
And, seizing the pen, he added the phrase
Which will honor his name to remotest days :
"Charles Carroll of Carrollton" now may we read,
And know 'twas none other that dared the brave deed.
Then he spake, as no coward or craven would dare :
"If George III wants Charles Carroll let him seek
    him there."

Charles Carroll of Carrollton, thou wert a man :
We honor thy spirit ;—though under the ban,
With a price on thy head if to liberty true,
While titles and honors were waiting for you,

If, a traitor to homeland, your voice you would lend
To the cause of the tyrant and cease to contend,
You stood up to be counted for freedom and right,
And threw down the gauntlet as Liberty's knight.

We want Carrolls today, men to do and to dare,
Who will stand up like heroes and take their full share
Of the danger and sacrifice they must e'er face
Who fearlessly strive for the weal of the race ;
Who in battle for right, though they stand all alone,
Yet, with hope anchored fast to eternity's throne,
Press in where the smoke and artillery peal
The need of true men and devotion reveal.

CUBA LIBRE.

Is the craving for freedom a crime now, forsooth,
That the tyrant turns loose his most bloodthirsty sleuth?
Are patriots beasts, to be taken and shot
For defending their rights 'gainst a devilish plot?
Shall heroes be bound by the gyves of the slave ;
And shall liberty yet find an ignoble grave
Within sight of the land that rejoiced in her birth,
And has forced all the world to acknowledge her worth ?

What has Cuba e'er asked that we asked not before?
'Tis the same boon we won mid the cannon's dull roar.
Shall the henchmen of tyrants pour in like a flood ?
Shall America's soil be enriched by the blood

Of the nobles of Cuba—far nobler than they
The dons of proud Spain who the tyrant obey—
While their cry of distress passes by us unheard,
And Columbia's statesmen protest not a word?

Nay; arouse ye, Columbia! Be yours the disgrace,
So deeply engraved time can never efface,
If, when struggling humanity, asking for naught
But the freedom for which our own forefathers fought,
Stands just at your door and for sympathy pleads
'Gainst the bloodhound of Spain, you ignore its great
    needs,
Surrender the cause you were born to maintain,
And permit patriot blood to be poured out in vain.

Let our solons forget each political broil
For a season, then hasten the butcher to foil;
Bid the murderous Spaniard forever to know
That when against freedom he dare strike a blow
'Neath Columbia's shadow, Columbia's flag
Is floating a-nigh, that 'tis not a base rag,
But to all the oppressed 'tis the flag of the free,
On America's main and her bordering sea.

BLUE-COAT JOE AND GRAY-COAT JOHN.

Two bronzed and gray-haired men into the war department came
With halting, feeble step, but eye with martial fire aflame.

The good right limb of one was gone; the other of
    his left,
Upon the field where flew the shell had some time
    been bereft.
Their wooden legs went clumping o'er the marble of
    the floor,
Their eyes scanned every opening to find the office
    door,
Across whose threshold orders went to armies near
    and far
Upon whose skill and bravery the nation leaned
    in war.

"Ah, John," said one, "I see it now, and there's the
    very one
I'd rather see today, my boy, than any 'neath the sun.
"Hello, there, general, don't you know this ornary
    rattle-head?
I charged with you at Petersburg; you left me there
    for dead.
You don't remember me, perhaps, for, 'mong the
    thousands more,
A private soldier hardly counts, they pass him light-
    ly o'er;
But I was pretty close to you until I headlong fell,
When Lee's men tripped my legs for me with that big
    piece of shell.

"I lost this leg at Petersburg, and John lost his there,
    too,
He fighting in the blown-out fort and I in charging
    through."

"I lost this leg at Petersburg, and John lost his there, too, He fighting in the blown-out fort and I in charging through."

"You see, 'twas just like this," said John, "we lived
   in Old Virginn,
And when the state seceded, sir, I thought it mortal sin
For any man to turn his back upon his native state
And let the love he bore to her be driven out by hate;
While Joe he thought the other way and said he
   couldn't see
The thing at all as I did, so we never could agree."

"You see," said Joe, "I reasoned that the only banner
   true
To which we owed our fealty was the proud red white
   and blue,
That when a state proved recreant and tried to trample it
Into the mire it ought to stir each man possessed of grit
To rouse in all his manhood and to draw th' avenging
   brand
To strike to earth the one who dares to raise an im-
   pious hand
Against the nation's sacred flag, the one our fathers
   brave
Had raised in honor on the land and o'er the ocean's
   wave.

"This couldn't last forever, so at last there came a day
When John and I our rifles took and each one marched
   away.
He turned him south, I hastened north, and each one
   found a place
Within the rival armies which soon brought us face
   to face.
He marched with Beauregard and I beneath McClellan
   fought,

And, while he strove to break the union, I for union wrought.
We did our best on either side, and each in his own way,
I dressed from top to toe in blue and he in rebel gray.

"At Gettysburg John charged on me—I thought I knew his phiz
When through the smoke he dashing came while we made bullets whiz.
I feared that he would surely drop for we hot volleys poured
From out our muskets in their face while loud our cannon roared;
But John seemed born to go between the balls which that day flew,
So he escaped the awful blast which there so deadly blew,
And, when Bob Lee marched south again, his army bruised and torn,
John kept his place with steady step though weary oft and worn."

"And so it went," said John again, "each did his level best
To help his side to knock the other clear to galley-west,
Sometimes Joe got the worst of it, sometimes he gave us fits,
Sometimes we both just socked it home and made some rattling hits.
But then at Petersburg, you see, we played the game too fine
When Grant that pesky tunnel dug and touched off that blamed mine.

I saw Joe coming for the breach ; I knew he meant
to take it,
In spite of all the great big guns that we could bring to
rake it.

"And Grant, too, made it fearful hot ; that breach he
fairly raked,
And 'neath the thunder of his guns the ground beneath
us quaked.
We jumped into the crater, sir, Joe's brave brigade
to stop,
And then the boys who wore the gray began to reel and
drop.
Then, sir, I caught a grape-shot where you see that
timber leg,
Which knocked the fight all out of me and took me
down a peg,
And first I knew Joe fell there, too—how strange is
war's caprice—
And that's the way we Gray and Blue each lost a leg
apiece."

"John's right in that,' said Joe again, "and now we're
both agreed
To march beneath 'Old Glory', sir, and see fair Cuba
freed.
We've only got a leg apiece, but they are seasoned well,
And if you give us two a chance we'll give them Span-
iards--well,
A taste of what they ought to've had a century ago,
For I can tell you, governor, those dons have got to go.

We've stumped it all the way from home on these old
    wooden pegs
To offer in the flag's defense our other two good legs."

"You see," said John, "I'm some ashamed of what I
    did before,
And now I'm anxious for a chance to wipe out that old
    score ;
I can't undo what has been done, and I'll not try, but then
Just put me down to fight beneath 'Old Glory' once again.
Joe flashed his powder in my face, and I in his flashed
    mine,
When he with Grant was in the trench and I in Bob
    Lee's line ;
But now we're going to elbow's touch and shoot the
    self-same way.
And neither one will ever tell that I once wore the gray."

PEACE.

I stood on the point of the mountain,
    And looked far over the plain,
Where once the beautiful valley
    Was cumbered with heaps of the slain ;
But I saw not the smoke of the battle,
    I heard not the sound of the strife,
There arose not the groans of the dying,—
    Aglow was all nature with life.

I saw the far off Chickamauga,
   In mem'ry recalled the dark day
When foemen charged backward and forward,
   Blood dyeing each foot of the way ;
But the streamlet flowed peacefully onward,
   Mid banks that were bordered with green,
And its waters reflected the sunshine,
   With bright, unadulterate sheen.

I gazed down the slope of the mountain,
   Where once the brave Hooker had led,
His men o'er the precipice climbing,
   The cloudy capped summit o'erhead ;
But the birds were now singing so sweetly,
   The mountain was elsewise so still,
That no one would dream how the cannon
   Had shaken each mountain and hill

Far below ran the beautiful river,
   The mountain engirt Tennessee,
Once covered with mortar and gunboat,
   To defend the true flag of the free ;
But there were no signs of the conflict,
   The steamers were brilliant and gay,
Ten thousand bright banners were flying,
   For leagues of the silvery way.

Before me I saw the vast thousands,
   All drawn up in martial array ;
In their midst stood the battle-scarred veterans,
   And mingled with them were the Gray :

But shoulder to shoulder they 'ligned them ;
  They swore to defend the same flag ;
And I caught the rich folds of "Old Glory,"
  Flung out from each mountain and crag.

Then high in the azure above them,
  In vision I saw a great light,
And the angel of peace on white pinions
  Just hovered in mid air so bright ;
While around her the heroes were gathered
  Who fell on that awful dark day ;
On a silvery cloud in the sunlight,
  They stood, clasping hands, Blue and Gray.

TAPS.

PART II.

SONGS OF THE HEART,

AND

COMMUNINGS WITH NATURE.

SONGS OF THE HEART.

HANG OUT THY LIGHT.

In the early part of the fifteenth century, before any system of street lighting had been adopted in London. the Mayor commanded that lanterns should be hung in front of each house. The watchmen, in passing their rounds, cried out to all delinquents, "Hang out your lights."

"Hang out thy light," the watchman cries,
"Art thou asleep? Thou must arise;
The street is dark before thy door;
The storm is wild—doth hear it roar?
Some hapless mortal, sinking here,
Will perish, e'en while home is near."

"Hang out thy light." 'Tis Christ's command;
Hold high thy lamp with steady hand;
The world's in darkness worse than night,
The world is lost without a light;
Canst thou thy lamp refuse, my child,
To light this dark and dreary wild?

Immortal souls are passing by,
Where perils hid before them lie ;
Their foes beset on every side ;
The pit of death yawns open wide ;
If thou withhold thy lamp a breath,
These souls may taste eternal death.

Gold greedy men, in league with hell,
Are watching now their souls to sell ;
False beacons gleam on every side ;
The doors of vice stand open wide ;
The glare of sin is shining bright ;
If thou wouldst save, hang out thy light.

Dost call thyself a child of God ?
All these were ransomed by His blood :
Think not, oh man, to guiltless be
If thou deny thy Master's plea ;
To rescue them from endless night,
Hang out thy light ! Hang out thy light !

Hang out thy light, nor suffer aught
To rob me of the souls I've bought ;
In bitter woe the price I paid,
A full atonement I have made
That each a fadeless crown might wear,
And in my future glory share.

Hang out thy light ; to thee is given
To guide the erring ones to heaven ;
Who these shall save, if, faithless, thou
Dost fail to keep thy solemn vow ?

Didst thou not promise mine to be,
To witness to the world for me?

Hang out thy light—What! Hast thou none?
Alas! the ransomed are undone;
Haste, let me breathe upon thy heart,
The sacred fire to thee impart;
Now hasten forth into the night,
To save the lost; hang out thy light.

RAISING OF LAZARUS.

And Lazarus was dead. His palsied heart
No longer urged the rich life current on;
His lips, that once had uttered words of love,
To those responsive which the sisters spoke,
The icy touch of death had frozen dumb;
Upon the happy home in Bethany,
Where oft the Son of man had rested Him
When weary 'neath the burdens which He bore,
Sorrow's cloud, surcharged with awful woe,
Had settled black as Egypt's darkness down.
Nor did th' occasion want a thing to cause
The clouds to take the deepest, darkest hue.
That home where Christ, the mighty Son of God,
So constant came as made it seem that His
All-powerful hand protected all within
Should open be to th' assaults of death,
Astonished all; and each, struck dumb, was mute.

Nor this the worst; for, e'en while life remained
To bid their flickering hope still burn,
A messenger was sent all haste to make
To him in whom they held full trust, and bid
Him come with all His healing power divine,
And speak the word that stopped the fever's course.

A hundred times had His all-powerful hand
Brought others help, when help no mortal saw;
Shall they, his truest friends, in vain appeal
When troubles like a mountain o'er them roll?
They would not so believe; they knew him true:
But, as the hours sped by and brought no word
From Him on whom their hope of help did rest,
They wondered; and their hearts were sorely pained,
That Christ came not their earnest call to heed,
But left them all alone in sore distress,
To fight, 'gainst fearful odds, a losing fight,
When he had power to turn the ebbing tide
Of life, and bid its current surging go
To arouse anew the wasted energies.
'Twas this, above all other woe, that weighed
Upon their souls on this eventful day;
That Jesus, in whose love their trusting hearts
Did rest with surest, sweetest confidence,
Should turn deaf ear to their despairing cry,
Was more than broken bleeding heart could bear.
But thus God oft withholds the blessing sought;
His child permits to reach the lowest depths
Of grief, or pain, or woe, or bitter loss;
That to these depths a hand divine may reach,
With blessings richer than it else might be,

And joy unspeakable at length bestow.
The sisters faithful stood until the end
Beside that bed of suffering and death,
Until the last short breath came gaspingly,
And Lazarus, the stay of both, was dead.

Then crushed they back the wailing cry of grief,
And bade prepare the body for the grave.
With spices, such as their poor purse could buy,
The form of him they held so dear, embalmed,
Lay stretched upon the couch where he had died.
From all the country round came many friends
To view the face of him they loved in life;
And then the funeral cortege wound its way
Among the hills that round sweet Bethany
Stand forth as sentinels to guard her hearths.
With heavy hearts the sisters followed on
To see the form of him so dearly loved
Entrusted to the tomb, there to await
The voice omnipotent and trumpet blast,
Which soon shall call the sleepers from the dust;
Soon! How soon ours it may not be to know;
But, as the one that ruleth all doth count,
The days are few, for he doth reckon time
By different scale of computation far
From that which we in finite wisdom use.
To him, a thousand years are but a day,
And, when 'tis past, it counts as yesterday
To us would seem, but just a trifling span
Of time In the eternal years of God.
To Martha, and to Mary, too, the time
When Lazarus should rise from out the sleep

Which held him locked in its secure embrace
So far away, so dim, so hidden seemed,
That faith alone, a strong, far reaching faith,
Could see him clothed with immortality,
A victor o'er the powers of death and hell.
And thus, when once the ponderous door was shut
Which closed the tomb and hid corruption's work,
They bid a long farewell to Lazarus,
And turned them sadly homeward once again.

What pen can e'er reveal the biting pain
Which lurked within their hearts for four long days?
The tendrils of their love so interwove,
And twined so closely round each tender heart,
And in the coils so many objects held,
That something, look which way they would, oft caught
And filled their thoughts with memories sweet of him,
To make unbearable his absence seem,
And burden each with sense of something lost.
The mother, she who drops the bitter tear
Upon the tiny shoe which meets her eye
While delving deep in long-forgotten place,
Can feel for them amid their awful woe ;
The wife, who sees upon the wall the face
Of him upon whose arm she proudly leaned,
Into whose face with confidence she looked
For many years,—Alas ! for years too short,—
Can tell why Martha's tears unbidden flowed,
E'en while her household cares were pressing her,
As, unexpectedly, some trifling thing

Which once her brother prized, her eyes beheld;
And why 'twas Mary oft would hide herself
In some secluded spot to think and weep,
As though her eyes, into a fountain turned,
Would deluge all the thirsty ground with tears.

And thus the days went dragging slowly by,
Until the morning of the fourth had dawned,
Since that, the dreariest day of all that they
Had ever known, though some had cloudy been.
Intent upon her household cares and work
Was Martha, Mary meanwhile standing by,
Her mind intent upon some memory,
When word there came that Christ himself drew
    near,
And soon would enter their beclouded home.
Then hastened Martha forth her Lord to meet
And pour her tale of woe into his ear,
With full assurance in his mighty power,
In hope—yet scarcely knowing what she hoped.
Though broken hearted, faith had bid expect
To hear such words of sympathy, as she
With hungry soul, so crushed by sorrows, craved.
Yet, as her eyes beheld him drawing nigh,
Her heart, that stubborn heart,'gainst him rebelled,
And poured she forth in bitter tones these words:
"Hadst thou been here my brother had not died."
And then her faith, triumphant over all,
Resumed its throne and once again she spake:
"But even now I know that God will grant
To thee whate'er thou findest faith to ask."
And then—how little understood was he?—

The Master said, "Thy brother shall arise."
"But only at the resurrection day,
When all who sleep beneath the sod shall rise,"
Blind unbelief bid Martha answer him ;
And, though the Lord declared his mighty power
To break the bonds of death and hell at will,
She blindly stood, nor grasped the assuring thought,
As Christ these words of confidence outspoke :
"I am the resurrection and the life."

Then Martha hastened back to Mary's side,
To bear to her the news that Christ had come,
And, coming, asked for her in tender tones.
But when the Master, full of sympathy,
The crushed and bleeding heart of Mary saw,
And how she wept, he in the spirit groaned,
Then asked where Lazarus, his friend, was laid,
That he might stand beside his grave and weep.
And weep? Ah, yes, he feeleth all our grief ;
His heart our heaviest, sorest burdens feels.
The man of sorrows, he our sorrows knows,
And bends in pity o'er each child of woe.
No tears are shed, no pains are ever borne,
Of which the Christ, the son of God knows not.
"And Jesus wept !"—ye suffering mortals, hear !
The Christ, the Father's equal on the throne
That high above the heavens majestic stands,
Shed tears of sympathy when mortals wept.
The bending heavens to earth and man came down,
When Christ that act of grace and pity did.
In sight of all the assembled hosts of heaven,
Who came a work of power divine to see,

The king of glory bowed his head and wept.
Stupendous sight! so human, yet divine!
Archangels wondering gathered him around,
And gazed in awe at sight so wondrous strange;
For none e'er saw a tear or heard a sigh
In that bright world from which the Saviour came,
Where seraphim no tears need ever shed;
But man, since sin its triumph o'er him won,
Most bitter tears has shed. And thus, when Christ,
Though Son of God divine, came man to save,
He stooped, his bitterest pangs of grief to share.
He knoweth all our cares, ah, blessed truth
To cheer us, else our burdened hearts would fail.
He wept, then turned to those who round him stood,
And bade remove the slab which closed the tomb;
But Martha, fearful to reveal the work
Of dissolution, quick objection made:
"My Lord, for four long days my brother lies
Within the tomb; a putrid mass must be
His body now, a foul offense to all.
Move not the stone, 'twill multiply our grief
To see corruption's work, and feel that he,
Our cherished one, lies rotting 'neath our gaze."

But Jesus answered: "Said I not to thee
God's glory thou shouldst see, if thou believe?"
Then lifted they the stone which o'er him lay,
And all the secrets of the grave were bare.
With reverent hearts they worshipped while he
    prayed,
As only he who knew the secret source
Of power divine omnipotent could pray.

In accents such as mortal tongue ne'er spake,
He lifted up his voice and thus addressed
The Father whose beloved Son he was:
"I thank Thee, Father, thou hast always heard,
Yet well I knew Thou never failst to hear;
But I would give such evidence complete,
That these and all whose souls I came to save,
Might know beyond a doubt Thou sendest me."

Full well He knew the great paternal love,
With open hand rich blessings to bestow,
Was yearning o'er the weeping, bleeding hearts
Which round the open tomb expectant stood.
He closed his prayer; approached the open door:
In voice that loudly echoed 'mong the hills,
The voice of One who knew His mighty power,
He called to him who slept the sleep of death,
"Come forth, dead Lazarus, make haste, come
    forth."
That voice the dormant energies aroused;
Its accents searched the hidden springs of life;
They woke the brain, and thrilled along the nerves;
In motion set the heart, sensation woke.
The frozen blood once more its course began,
And flowed a healthy stream and bearing life
From center to circumference around;
The flush of health death's pallor drove away;
The eye, long glazed and set and blind,
Its curtains lifted and let in the light,
Gave one quick look, and rested on the face
Of him who called, then sparkled with a gleam
Of recognition glad, and Lazarus rose;

And he, once dead, came forth all bound about
With linen cloths, the tomb's habiliments.
The grave no depths possessed beyond the reach
Of that almighty power incarnate there.
The conqueror, death, his conquest yielded up,
When Christ, the all victorious God, appeared.
Then old Judea's hills re-echoed round
The shouts of joy, the songs of praise to him
Who, having given life, had taken it,
That He the joy of each might multiply
By life returned, a more abundant life.

What pen can e'er describe, what painter's brush
Depict the rapturous joy the sisters knew,
As to their bursting hearts they once again
Pressed Lazarus, snatched anew from death's
  embrace,
And given in all his manhood back again,
To cheer their way and walk a little while
The rough and rugged path of life with them?
Stupendous miracle! divinely wrought!
Which brings the bodies of the dead to life,
Death's sting removes, the grave of victory robs!
Thus shall it be when time shall be no more,
And comes the glorious resurrection morn;
Not one who sleeps beneath the waving grass,
Not one above whose bed the billows roll,
So far remote or so obscure shall be,
That Christ may not the dead arouse to life;
But, though they lie ten thousand fathoms deep,
Though winds their dust have scattered far and wide,
That searching voice the deepest depths shall sound,

Shall call the dust from earth's remotest bound,
Until each atom finds its scattered mates,
And, washed, and clothed with immortality,
These bodies, here with sin defiled,
Shall, death's dominion o'er, inherit life.

WAITING FOR JESUS.

"For they were all waiting for Him."—Luke viii-40.

Forth on a mission of mercy
  Jesus, the Saviour was gone,
Over the sea to Gadara,
  Healing the legion cursed one.
Back from the conflict returning,
  Victor o'er power of hell,
Thousands were waiting with greeting
  Him whom their hearts loved so well.

Where human burdens were greatest,
  When once His presence was sought,
Patiently doing His bidding,
  Joy for each sorrow He brought,
Thus came the multitude thronging—
  Long had they waited for Him,
Wondering why He thus tarried
  Looking till eyes had grown dim.

Here sat the pale-cheeked woman,
　　She of the issue of blood,
She with the nature so timid,
　　Yearning to meet with her Lord.
Still shrank she back from the others,
　　Hiding from all her sore need,
Hoping and praying, yet fearing
　　Jesus her cry would not heed.

Fain would she run from His presence,
　　Dreading rebuke or rebuff—
How could she ever endure it?
　　Her burdens were surely enough.
Faith said, "Fear not, He will heal you;"
　　Doubt, "Your case he will not treat;"
Need cried, "He must not refuse me;
　　If so, I'll die at his feet.'

Daughter of Jairus lay dying,
　　Beautiful light of his home,
Oh! that the Master might hasten,
　　E'er her pure spirit had flown.
There stands the man and the ruler,
　　Straining his eyes o'er the sea,
Helpless to succor the dear one—
　　Waiting for Christ with His plea.

Short grew the breath of the maiden,
　　Lying so white on her bed.
Soon, with a gasp, it was ended,
　　The maid's lovely spirit had fled.

Still stood her father, unknowing
    Death had the victory won,
Straining his eyes o'er the gloaming,
    Waiting for Mary's great son.

Here were the blind, halt and palsied,
    Each with his sickness to heal,
Lovingly, anxiously waiting
    Him who their sorrow could feel.
Oh, the great burdens they carried!
    Wondering why He came not;
Asking each other so often,
    "Will He not pity our lot?"

See yonder group on the hillside,
    Far from the crowd on the beach,
Holding aloof from the others,
    Far away out their reach.
Those are the lepers, the outcasts,
    Driven to live in the caves,
Waiting for death to come slowly,
    Or plunging to death in the waves.

Many another was waiting,
    Waiting the Master to greet,
Bringing some heart-crushing burden,
    With which to fall at His feet.
Many the heartaches that waited
    Yonder on Galilee's shore,
Waited, yes anxiously waited
    Him who to cure them had power.

See ; far out on the billows,
   See yonder snowy white sail ;
Or is it only a seabird
   Dipping its wing in the swell?
No ; it is Jesus that's coming,
   Bringing a blessing for all.
None who have waited for Jesus
   Ever in vain for Him call.

He who knows best his own purpose
   Never too late will draw nigh ;
Though to us waiting, the moments
   Seem to drag heavily by.
Lepers shall lose their uncleanness ;
   Blind men with clearness shall see ;
Lame ones shall leap in their gladness ;
   Death from His presence shall flee.

Jesus is still the same Saviour,
   Loving and gentle and true ;
Coming each day to our hearthstones,
   Coming our joys to renew.
Sometimes he seems long to tarry ;
   Sometimes we weary become ;
But, e'er our burden o'erwhelm us,
   If we but trust, He will come.

Are you now waiting, my brother,
   Trusting your all to His care?
Jesus has gone to His kingdom
   For you a house to prepare.

But He will never forget you,
　　Though He wait long by the way ;
Soon He will come in His beauty,
　　Bringing the brightness of day.

Your dearest hopes may have perished,
　　Hopes that were light to your soul,
Leaving the blackness of darkness
　　Over your spirit to roll.
Jesus, the glorified Saviour,
　　Can, with the voice of command,
Reaching the depths of that darkness,
　　Call the lost hopes to thy hand.

DOT'S LOVE LETTER.

"I'se w'itin' a letter, deah papa, to 'ou,
A p'ecious, sweet love-letter,—full of it, too.—
Don't 'ou wish 'ou could see 'ou' own mischievous
　　dirl ?—
My ! what a bid word, how it makes my head whirl—
But I love 'ou, deah papa, wid all o' my heart ;
It is not vewy bid, but 'ou own evwy part ;
Yes, an' mamma, s'e owns it, too, evwy mite,
An' I dess 'are's enough for 'ou both, or mos' quite.

"How I wish 'ou had tum up 'e pathway today
While I was out un'er 'e shade trees at play,
I would dess runned an' smovered 'ou wid a bid tiss—
Wouldn't 'at be dess jolly ? Let me tell 'ou dis',

When a dirl, like 'e one 'at 'ou talls 'ittle Dot,
Has such a nice papa, s'e love him a lot;
An' mine is 'e bes' papa un'er 'e sun ;—
If I tould des' see him, now wouldn't I run?

"An' I dess 'ou'd run, too, I know 'ou would lot
When 'ou saw 'at 'e 'ittle dirl tummin' was Dot.
Den 'are'd be a tollission—ma says 'at's 'e word—
Out 'are near 'e maple 'at stands in 'e yard,
An' I'd do for 'our pocket 'ou better des' bet,
To see what 'ou'd dot 'are an' what I tould det.
I 'spect it 'ould be a nice dolly, don't 'ou?
Wid eyes 'at tould shut, an' a dwess lightes' blue.

"My kittie is sp'endid; 'ou dess' ough' to see
Us a chasin' each ozer as fast as tould be;
S'e tatches my ball an' runs un'er 'e bush,
An' 'en out s'e dumps an' does off on 'e rush.
I wish I tould tell 'ou about all 'e res'
But my head des' teeps dwappin' tlear down on my
    bweast.
Deah mamma is bwingin' my nighty so white
I'se so awful s'eepy; mus' tiss 'ou dood night.

I LOOKED IN HER EYES.

I looked in her eyes, and what do you think?
Say, what do you think in their depths were revealed?
Now, whether her eyes were far blacker than ink,
Or as ocean depth blue, or light gray, was concealed.

And, though it seem strange, I must surely confess
That as to their color I dare not e'en guess ;
For, so great were their depths, so transparent their hue,
That I never saw one who could say that he knew.

But I saw—well, now, really, you might not see
What I'm sure that I saw there 'neath the oak tree :
While the moon, looking down from the clear stellar
    space,
Pulled a soft, fleecy cloud up in front of her face,
Lest she, too, might chance from the heavens to see
What I'm sure that my true love meant only for me ;
And, e'er on a zephyr the cloud sped away,
I had learned what those eyes to my soul would fain say.

But you ask me again what so brilliantly shone
On that bright moonlight eve in the eyes of my love,
As she placed her soft hand with full trust in my own,
And looked up in my face her devotion to prove.
But 'tis useless to ask ; you have no right to know
What I saw in her eyes, what I pressed on her brow ;
For no other e'er saw, no other will see
What those beautiful eyes then revealed unto me.

THE SILVER ANNIVERSARY.

It is twenty-five years, little sweet-heart, today,
We've been trav'ling together o'er life's checkered way.
    We've had crosses to bear,
    Many blessings to share ;

And so happy were we, and our lives did so blend,
We forgot when our honeymoon came to an end :
  So, with royal good will,
  We are keeping it still ;
And no groom at the altar e'er stood by his bride
Half so proudly as I stand today by your side.

How swiftly time flies ! And how short the years seem !
They are gone with the speed of our thoughts as we dream:
  Those silvery years,
  Those beautiful years ;
And, as memory's scroll is unrolled to my sight,
I wonder, dear wife, as I stand here to-night,
  How the Father above,
  In His infinite love,
Could have found me a blessing on this side of heaven
Half so rich as your love which to me he has given.

It has not been all sunshine, ah no, but behind
Every cloud that hung o'er us the sun ever shined ;
  And through rifts we could see
  How much richer 'twould be
When the Father's kind hand brushed the curtain aside.
But, if sunshine were granted, or if 'twere denied,
  We were happy together
  In all changes of weather ;
For love, though it thrives in the warmest sunlight,
By its presence makes even the gloomy day bright.

We could surely accomplish an immense sight more
If we had the whole twenty-five years to live o'er :
  But that shows on the whole
  We're not overly dull ;

And we've learned a few things to bequeath to our son
That we can't say we knew when our trip was begun ;
        In experience we're rich.
        If there has been some hitch
In piling up ducats, green, yellow or white,
And though often our purse has been painfully light.

For the many kind friends of the years that are gone ;
For those that are here, for those that are you ;
        For the old, for the new,
        For each one that's been true,
We've a grasp of the hand as we tarry today
To recall the loved forms we have passed on our way.
        May no evil betide,
        But may love e'er abide ;
May their clouds melt away 'neath the sunlight's bright
    glow
And their barks ever sail where the gentlest winds blow.

And now we are taking our bearings today,
E'er we try what ahead may lie hid by the way ;
        And we're trimming our sails
        For fair weather or gales
That in years yet before us may buffet our craft ;
Yet we pray that kind breezes our ship may e'er waft,
        Till in harbor above,
        Home of infinite love,
We shall anchor at last where no storms ever roar,
And with joy disembark on eternity's shore.

SHIP AHOY!

Ship ahoy! Where art thou sailing?
    Outward bound?
Dost thou know the dangers lying
    All around?

See yon headlight on the starboard;
    Note it well.
Steer thy course far out to larboard
    Shun the swell.

Hear you not the breakers pounding
    On the rocks,
All the air around resounding
    With the shocks?

Ship ahoy! Ahoy!! Ahoy there!!!
    Death you court!
Follow not that false decoy, there,
    Hard aport!

Siren voices bid you tarry
    By the way.
Heed them not; be wary, wary,
    All the day.

"Ship ahoy!" thy Pilot calls thee,
    Drifting by;
Turn to me, if sin enthralls thee;
    I am nigh."

Ship far out on ocean sailing,
    Full of joy ;
List your Saviour's voice now hailing,
    "Ship ahoy !

"Pleasure's maelstrom's round you whirling
    Wild and free,
E'er you sink beneath the swirling,
    Flee to me."

Art thou on the ocean driving,
    Tempest tossed,
Hurricanes thy mainsail riving,
    Compass lost,

Sorrows billows o'er thee rolling
    Mountain high ?
Jesus Christ, the sea controlling,
    Passeth by.

Crowd on sail with dauntless ardor,
    Tempest tried ;
Keep your course straight toward the harbor,
    God your guide.

Ship ahoy, we've reached the haven,
    Dangers past,
Cast the anchor, God hath given
    Heaven at last.

THE MEADOW LARK.

Tinkle-linkle-loo!
Meadow lark so true;
First in spring of all, his singing,
As his soul he doth outpour,
Best good cheer to each one bringing,
Tells that winter's reign is o'er.

Tinkle-linkle-loo!
Up, be up and do.
Thus his cheery morning greeting
Echoes from the meadow nigh,
While his mate, his challenge meeting,
Linkle loo! pipes loud near by.

Tinkle-linkle-o-o-lee!
Hear him sing on yonder tree,
Happy in the sun of morning,
Quick he gives a flip his tail,
Then, without a note of warning,
Drops him down upon a rail.

Loo-o-tinkle-o-o-lee!
Who can sing more merrily?
Watch his nervy, graceful motion;
See him as he struts around,
Pacing, hopping, as the notion
Suits him best, upon the ground.

O-lee-o-tinkle-lee !
Oh see, come quick and see ;
Here's a worm or two for luncheon ; —
Down upon them comes his bill ;
Soon we hear contented munching ;
Then he flies off o'er the hill

Lee-o-tinkle-linkle !
Let your music tinkle ;
Bird of cheery note so varied,
Singing sweetly all the day,
Always busy, never wearied,
Welcome with your roundelay.

Lee-o-tinkle-lee !
Sing, bright bird, to me ;
None too oft we hear your trilling ;
Hourly let your notes ascend
Toward the skies, all bosoms thrilling,
Meadow lark, our merry friend,

Lee-o-tinkle o-o-lee !
Thou dost cause our doubts to flee.
Prophet thou of coming harvest,
Trustful in the heaven above,
He hath sent thee thus to give us
Faith in Him, the God of love.

INTO THE FURNACE.

"Come, Shadrach, bow down 'fore the great brazen god ;
And, Meshach, your knee, too, must touch the green sod ;
Abednego, prostrate yourself on the ground ;
See the thousands of Babylon lying around."
      But with courage sublime,
      Which has challenged all time,
The three made reply: "Though we honor the king,
We can never consent to so wicked a thing
As to offer to that senseless pile what alone
Is due to the one on eternity's throne."

"Seven times what is wont," the mad king fiercely cried,
"Heat the furnace for them, lest they quickly decide
When the cornet, the flute, harp, and dulcimer sound,
To prostrate themselves on their face to the ground
      And the image adore,
      While they promise no more
The king's will to resist, but to worship each day,
The great god he has made and set up by the way."
But the men gave him answer: "If God's will it be,
We will die in the furnace, but yield not to thee."

See the smoke rolling forth from yon ponderous pile,
While the proud monarch's lips curl in cynical smile ;
And his willing slaves jest as they feed the hot fire,
To prepare for God's children a funeral pyre.
      But how vain every plan
      Of the mightiest man,

Which ignores the great Father who rules over all,
Attentive to hear every needy one's call ;
An imbecile he, though a king on the throne,
Who e'er dares fight against the Omnipotent One.

While their eyes blaze with hatred, the minions of law
Hurl the faithful three into the fiery maw
Of the furnace, now melting with sevenfold heat,
As the fiercely red tide on brazen doors beat.
      But the flames, so well fed,
      Strike the king's soldiers dead,
While the chains, melted off, drop all shapeless and prone,
And the three are beheld, standing safe and alone—
Ah, no ! not alone, for in robes like the sun,
The king by their side saw the Glorified One.

Does the furnace, my brother, yawn hot in thy sight,
While the foes to thy peace tower strong in their might?
Do the fierce, scorching billows tumultuous roll
And o'erwhelm with dismay thy faint, fear-stricken soul?
      In that furnace walks He
      Who once died on the tree ;
And who leaneth on Him in the midst of the fire,
Though the hatred-fed flames rise e'er higher and higher,
Shall come forth all unscathed without even the smell
Of the flames, though they're fed from the caverns of hell.

LAKE MICHIGAN.

There rolls, far, far from ocean's tide,
From great Atlanta's vistas wide,
   Mid woody hills embowered,
A lake of broad immensity,
And darksome depths, an inland sea,
   With mighty forces dowered ;
Its rolling billows in their sweep,
Its cliff-girt shore, its caverns deep,
   Old coral reefs among :
Its vast expanse, more lovely far
Than mountain dales, its beauty rare
   Inspire the poet's song.
When gentle zephyrs kiss the waves,
They softly roll until they lave
   The beach with softest purling,
Or, gathered into one long swell,
They rise and fall with cadence still,
   Without a ripple's curling ;
But when the storm cloud's marshalled host
Charge o'er the waters they are tossed
   And hurled aloft, till, falling,
They break, a thousand drops of spray,
Or strike the good ship on her way,
   With Titan force appalling.
Oh, mighty deep, at times so calm,
When wintry winds disturb thy realm,
   Thy awful power revealing,

The sounding crash and awful roar
Of breakers dashing on the shore
   Outvies the thunder's pealing.
A hapless fate the vessel meets,
Against whose hull thy fury beats,
   Amid the thunder's crashing ;
She groans, she writhes, she climbs the steep,
   Then plunges sheer into the deep,
   Her crew to ruin dashing.

Where lies Alpena's battered hull,
That once, as sprightly as the gull,
   Danced o'er the waves so lightly?
What caverns deep her timbers hide,
Far down below the swelling tide,
   Mid slime and ooze unsightly?
Her crew, who made such gallant fight,
When howled the hurricane that night,
   And starward heaved the billows,
To loving friends shall ne'er return ;
Thy caverns deep their ashes urn ;
   Thy sands are now their pillows.
Oh, gruesome night, when from the port
This good old ship had sallied forth,
   Her cabin human freighted
With four score souls, a joyous band,
While friends on shore each wave the hand,
   None dreaming what was fated.
Out from the port, mid mirth and song,
From those upon the deck who throng,
   The gallant vessel pushes;
But soon, ah, soon, the songs are stilled,

Each gleesome note by terror chilled,
　　While water o'er her rushes.
No soul returns to tell the tale,
How, mid the tempest's dismal wail,
　　That gallant crew and daring,
For life fought on throughout the night,
Yet doomed at last to lose the fight,
　　The ship's destruction sharing.

In days gone by, these placid waves
Were plowed by craft of savage braves,
　　And o'er the lake resounding,
The warwhoop fierce defiance bore,
Which echoed back from nearest shore
　　As, yonder headland rounding,
There swiftly came a rival fleet,
With courage manned the foe to meet,
　　His utmost strength defying.
The Foxes doubled on their tracks,
When on the wave they met the Sacs,
　　And soon were homeward flying.
The Chippewas and Ojibiways
Upon the lake had many frays,
　　When, in a horrid medley,
And hand to hand, with savage cheers,
They hurled their tomahawks and spears
　　And rained their arrows deadly.
Their echoing yells reverberate
Along the shore without abate,
　　Hurled backward o'er the water
From 'gainst the cliffs and wooded shore,
With din above the breakers' roar,

The while the strife grows hotter.
The air is darkened with the cloud
Of flying bolts. The leader proud,
　In crest of darkest raven,
His dusky warriors onward cheers,
Himself a stranger to the fears
　That pale the cheek of craven.
The birchen ships are lashed abreast,
As, riding on the swell's high crest,
　Their prows come onward dashing ;
Their ribs with blood are spattered red,
Their decks are strewn with warriors dead,
　As through their brains go crashing
The war-club, swung by demon hate,
And downward borne with all the weight
　Of strength and fury savage.
The scalping knife the work completes ;
Each yelling brave his comrade greets ;
　Their homes are saved from ravage.
The rolling wave soon washes out
All signs of battle and of rout,
　And quiet reigns supremely ;
The smiling sun looks kindly down
Upon the lake and headland brown,
　Benignly and serenely.

In age more dim what people strange
Along thy shores were wont to range,
　And claim this vast dominion ?
No monarch owned a wider sway ;
No eagle, though for many a day
　He flew on rapid pinion,

Could compass all their empire great,
Though swift he flew without abate ;
  For, labor worn and weary,
Long days e'er half his task were done,
His strength full spent, would he sink down,
  Or haste to seek his eyrie.
From north to south it stretched away,
Throughout that paradise where lay
  The Mississippi valley.
Along the shores of that great flood,
They lived in peaceful quietude
  Or met in warlike rally.
Their city walls, each templed hill
Declare their mighty power still,
  And there, with service mystic,
They worshipped God, to them unknown ;
They bowed in awe before his throne,
  The blazing sun majestic.

Where proud Chicago regal stands,
Upon the lakeshore's ancient sands,
  In all her power Titanic,
This ancient race held lighter sway,
And hence they launched their ships away,
  Or fled the storm in panic.
'Twas here they brought the brazen ore,
From Lake Superior's distant shore,
  And then, the streamlets threading,
They homeward bore the precious freight,
Their temple shrines to decorate,
  Where human blood was shedding.
Where now we tread these shores along,

The groves once echoed with the song
  Of lovely Toltec maiden;
Where mighty steamships plow the wave,
In tiny craft their seamen brave
  Returned with treasure laden;
Their homeward song, when far away,
Came o'er the waves and up the bay,
  Where, waiting, were the lasses
With laughing eyes so deep and dark,
And voices sweet as meadow lark,
  And raven-tinted tresses.
Mysterious race! so fully fled!
What secret charnel holds thy dead?
  Where sleep thy princes noble?
What awful besom swept the land?
What vandals dared, with ruthless hand,
  To bring this direful trouble?
The red man came and stood amazed,
As on the lofty mounds he gazed,
  In solitude unbroken;
The vanquished race he sought in vain,
O'er bounding wave and wooded plain;
  They gave of them no token.

Then came at length the paler race,
To claim the empire and efface
  The works of people olden;
To bid the land to lavish forth
Its richest gifts from south to north,
  And yield its fruitage golden.
Behold the lake's transforming now;
What stately ships her billows plow,

By wind and vapor driven!
What though the tempest in its wrath
Builds barriers 'thwart the steamship's path!
   What though, with thunder riven,
The storm cloud lifts its threatening head,
And, swooping down with direful spread,
   Turns loose the hurricane!
She laughs at storm, the billows spurns;
Her heart of fire more redly burns,
   And on she drives amain.

Along the shore great cities rise,
Their high walls towering toward the skies,
   Like those of ancient Babel.
May wisdom's counsels govern all,
Lest these great marts to ruin fall
   Like Babel's tower unstable.
Where warrior chieftains once controlled,
And chased the deer throughout the wold,
   Or war-cries fiercely shouted,
The merchant now the scepter bears;
The diadem he proudly wears
   While Indian braves are routed.
On boards of trade he plies his art,
Fictitious values to impart,
   To corn and wheat and barley.
To fortunes gain where others lose,
Men practice every feint and ruse,
   And shout both late and early.
When bull meets bear all bedlam's out,
And devil's wandering free about,
   While pandemonium rages.

With yells and growls the air resounds,
From vaulted roof the din rebounds,
   As bull with bear engages.
From scenes like these we gladly fly,
To list the lake's soft lullaby,
   As, o'er the pebbles gliding,
The rippling waves, with music sweet,
Break into spray just at our feet,
   Their sands to us confiding.
Oh, rolling deep! Oh, mighty sea!
Thy murmuring waters speak to me,
   Amid life's cares perplexing;
They speak my troubled soul to calm,
In softest accents like a balm,
   To heal the wound that's vexing.
Thou hast a voice for every mood,
If at thine ebb, or at thy flood,
   To all my soul appealing.
Thou speak'st to me in joyful hours,
Or when the cloud of sorrow lowers,
   To me sweet comfort dealing.
Roll on, oh deep, in sweep sublime,
From present to the latest time,
   In all thy varied splendor!
Lie peaceful 'neath the moonlight's glow;
Or, when the mighty tempests blow,
   Heave wild with awful grandeur.

THE REVOLT IN THE MUSEUM.

The professor sat back in his great easy chair
At the close of the day in his strangely built lair ;
Not a sound to disturb where an hour before
He had heard murm'ring voices, a thousand or more.
On the table lay corms, culms and bulbs piled about
In confusion confounded, a desperate rout ;
While the skeleton, hung in the closet near by,
Grinned a horrible grin at the weary man's sigh.

The monster stuffed owl made the curator shrink.
Staring into his eyes without motion or wink ;
While the open-mouthed lynx purred and snarled to himself,
As he glared at the pheasant on opposite shelf ;
And the powerful puma seemed poised for a spring
At the lovely gazelle, just to left of the wing
Of the hovering eagle, which motionless soared
O'er the whole great museum attached to a board.

A covey of quails, looking timidly out
From a nice quiet corner, saw, spying about,
A big shaggy fox with his nose to the ground
And his ears both pricked up to take in every sound.
"Everything seems alert," the professor remarked—
He was sure that the coyote his head turned and barked·
Then the big spotted loon gave a dolorous cry,
As a flock of stuffed pigeons flew merrily by.

From the jars on the shelves jumped a score of green
    frogs,
So drunk that not one could quite sit on a log :
For each was with alcohol prime so full soaked
That their tongues were all thick and their throats
    only croaked ;
For all of the world like the human biped
Who, like any fool, takes it into his head
That the stuff which is good frogs and serpents to
    pickle
Is well calculated his fancy to tickle.

"A convention is called, it is easy to see,"
Quoth the Prof., squinting out 'neath the lid of his 'e' ;
Then he quietly sat with his eyelids near closed
And pretended, the scamp, that he really dozed :
For he thought that in this way he'd surely find out
What all the commotion around was about.
He knew something portentious was down on the
    docket
When he saw a stuffed ape close the door and fast
    lock it.

"And now," quoth Judge Owl, "let the court come
    to order ;
Bring forward the culprit to plead, Mr. Warder;
At the bar let him stand and show cause if he can
Why he placed his own relatives under the ban.
He says that he comes of a pedigree old
That runs back twenty millions of years, I am told,
The tadpole, our cousin, the story once ran,
Evoluted his tail and turned into a man.

"I am not yet quite sure that I quote him correctly,
For I have not followed him so circumspectly
That I can quite give his pet theory complete,
And name all the steps that led up to the feat
Which put on a pollywog such a thick head
As this worldly-wise mortal will carry to bed."
"But I have his own word," brayed a lopsided donkey,
"That there sits a tail-less, degenerate monkey."

"What's that?" cried a pigmy who came from the
    south,
As he squinted his eyes and wide opened his mouth,
"Do you dare to insult me by claiming that I
Am related to him? Who invented the lie?"
Then the mite danced about and kept chatt'ring away
Till 'twas plain to be seen there was mischief to pay.
The curator wondered what he could have done,
While querying whether to stay or to run.

But e'en as he waited the room was in motion,
And the inmates were chasing about as the notion
Possessed them. The fox tried the rabbit to worry;
The hawk kept the quails in a tremulous flurry;
While the butcher bird, seizing an innocent wren,
Hung it high on a thorn just in front of his den;
And a watersnake, grabbing a jubilant frog,
Gulped him down in a trice and then lay like a log.

Pandemonium loose, devils on a rampage,
Could scarce equal in fury the animal rage.
The picture the room and the inmates then made
No counterpart has but the great boards of trade,

Where the bulls and the bears in confusion complete,
Each strives to make markets for corn and for wheat,
While, the whole big menag'rie turned loose on the town,
The big catch the little and gobble them down.

Just then the scared Prof., falling out of his chair,
Gave his head such a bump on a rockery near
That he woke with a start and lay staring around,
His brain in a whirl, amid silence profound.
The sun in the west was just sinking from sight,
Throwing over each form the first shadows of night ;
And he thought a broad grin cantered over the face
Of the monster stuffed ape as he turned from the place.

LEND A HAND.

Lend a hand, Brother Jones, to that man in the gutter :
    He fell in the pit that you dug
When you went to the polls alongside the big brewer
    And voted the same as the thug.
Lift him out of the hole and then help us to fill it—
    "With prayers ?" No, you've learned them by rote,
No answer you'll get while the devil hobnobbing ;
    You must help fill that hole with your vote.

It is whiskey has downed more than all else beside, sir,
    Distillers just laugh at your prayers ;
The way to lift him an' keep others from fallin'
    Is to close all the devilish lairs.

Your petitions ne'er reach to your own humble ceilin',
    They climb not the heavenly way ;
If you wish them in heaven to waken the echoes,
    You surely must vote as you pray.

Jesus Christ has no use for a man that's a dodger,
    Who to stand for the right is afraid,
Who thinks that for temp'rance he does his whole duty,
    If he stands now and then on parade.
If the battle is won, there are blows to be given ;
    Each man his whole duty must do,
In the home and in public, on rostrum, in pulpit,
    And prove at the ballot box true.

You may skirmish about and the field reconnoiter,
    An' startle a moment the foe,
By firin' a shot now an' then an' retreatin'
    Lest some party leader may know ;
But no soldier e'er won either vict'ry or honor
    Who faced not the foe to the last ;
An' you too will do naught that will count lest you hasten
    Your vote 'gainst the devil to cast.

He's he funny old codger, is old Mr. Satan,
    An' likes to crack practical jokes,
An' he shouts till he sets hell's high arches to ringing,
    An' he laughs an' he laughs till he chokes,
When he sees the procession of preachers an' brewers
    An' deacons an' bummers an' pimps
An' stewards, class leaders and Sunday school teachers,
    Each voting as told by his imps.

HELP HIM WHEN HE'S DOWN.

It costs such a mite we are always quite ready
  To help in prosperity's smile ;
And it tickles our pride that a hand we are lendin'
  To him who has made a big pile ;
But it's when his lank pocket contains not a dollar,
  And grocer's bills trouble his dreams ;
It is then that a hand, sir, reached down to a brother
  Makes friendship be all that it seems.

When a feller is nigh to the top of the ladder
  An' goin' it hand over hand,
He cares not a groat for your freely made offer
  To give him a boost on demand ;
It is not the best time, sir, to be so officious,
  Remember 'tis not now your say ;
He can reach the top round with an ease that's far greater
  If you will keep out of his way.

It is when somethin's happened an' losin' his balance ;
  His feet from the runnel both slip ;
Or he plunges to earth like a burnt out ol' rocket,
  His hands having lost all their grip,—
It is then that he needs the strong grasp of a brother,
  Backed up by a brother's warm heart,
To help him to rise and to get a new foot-hold
  With courage to make a new start.

www.ingramcontent.com/pod-product-compliance
Lightning Source LLC
Chambersburg PA
CBHW020255170426
43202CB00008B/385